DON'T TELL THE PRI

Patrick Weller is professor of politics and public policy, and the director of the Centre for Australian Public Sector Management at Griffith University in Queensland. He has studied life at the top in Australia and other parliamentary countries for the past 25 years. Among his books are *Can Ministers Cope?* (with Michelle Grattan); *First Among Equals: Prime Ministers in Westminster Systems*; *Malcolm Fraser PM*; *Dodging Raindrops: John Button, A Labor Life*; and *Australia's Mandarins: The Frank and the Fearless?*. He is writing a history of the Australian cabinet from 1901 to 2001.

SCRIBE SHORT BOOKS

A series of fresh perspectives on important developments in Australian society, culture, and politics

Series editors:
Peter Browne and Julian Thomas
Institute for Social Research
Swinburne University of Technology

Don't Tell the Prime Minister

Patrick Weller

Scribe Publications
Melbourne

Scribe Publications Pty Ltd
PO Box 523
Carlton North, Victoria, Australia 3054
Email: scribe@bigpond.net.au

First published by Scribe Publications 2002

Copyright © Patrick Weller 2002

All rights reserved. Without limiting the rights under copyright reserved above, no part of this publication may be reproduced, stored in or introduced into a retrieval system, or transmitted, in any form or by any means (electronic, mechanical, photocopying, recording or otherwise) without the prior written permission of both the copyright owner and the above publisher of this book.

Typeset in 11 on 14pt Minion by Peter Browne
Printed and bound in Australia by Griffin Press

National Library of Australia
Cataloguing-in-Publication data

Weller, Patrick, 1944- .
 Don't tell the prime minister.
 ISBN 0 908011 76 8.

 1. Australia. Parliament - Elections, 2001. 2. Administrative responsibility - Australia. 3. Refugees - Government policy - Australia. 4. Illegal aliens - Government policy - Australia. 5. Political campaigns - Australia. 6. Australia - Politics and government - 1990- . I. Title.

 352.350994

www.scribepub.com.au

Contents

Cast of characters   vi

1. What the public was told   1

2. Behind the scenes   8

3. Does our system work?   51

4. Accountability and Australian government   92

Sources   103

Acknowledgements   104

Cast of characters

Prime Minister's Office
John Howard, Prime Minister
Arthur Sinodonis, Chief of Staff
Miles Jordana, International Affairs Adviser

Prime Minister's Department
Max Moore-Wilton, Secretary
Jane Halton, Deputy Secretary and Chair of Taskforce
Katrina Edwards, First Assistant Secretary, Social Policy Division
Jennifer Bryant, Assistant Secretary, Social Policy Division and author of the internal report on the affair
Dr Brendon Hammer, Assistant Secretary, Intelligence and Security Branch, International Division
Harinder Sidhu, Senior Adviser, Intelligence and Security Branch
Commander Stefan King, Defence Liaison, Intelligence and Security Branch

Minister of Defence's Office
Peter Reith, Minister for Defence
Peter Hendy, Chief of Staff
Mike Scrafton, Defence Adviser
Ross Hampton, Media Adviser

Defence Department
Dr Allan Hawke, Secretary
Jenny McKenry, Head, Public Affairs and Corporate Communications Division (PACC)
Brigadier Gary Bornholt, Defence Liaison, PACC

CAST OF CHARACTERS

Australian Defence Force
Admiral Chris Barrie, Chief of Defence Force
Air Marshal Angus Houston, Chief of Air Force
Vice Admiral David Shackleton, Chief of Navy
Air Vice Marshal Alan Titheridge, Head, Strategic Command,
Rear Admiral Chris Ritchie, Commander Australian Theatre
Rear Admiral Geoffrey Smith, Maritime Commander
Brigadier Michael Silverstone, Commander Joint Taskforce, Darwin
Group Captain Steve Walker, Strategic Command and member of the People Smuggling Taskforce
Commander Norman Banks, Captain of HMAS *Adelaide*

Immigration Minister's Office
Philip Ruddock, Minister for Immigration

Department of Immigration
Bill Farmer, Secretary

Senate Select Committee on a Certain Maritime Incident
Peter Cook, Chair, Labor
John Faulkner, Labor Leader of the Opposition in the Senate
Jacinta Collins, Labor
George Brandis, Liberal
Brett Mason, Liberal
Alan Ferguson, Liberal
Andrew Bartlett, Democrat

CHAPTER 1
What the public was told

The image was unforgettable and horrifying. Refugees were throwing their children overboard. They wanted to force Australian sailors to rescue them and land them on Australian shores. They were desperate not to be sent back to the embattled countries from which they had fled. Just two days into the election campaign, government ministers grabbed the opportunity to drive home to the electorate the necessity for protecting the borders, particularly from people who would stoop so low as to risk the lives of their children.

Within hours of the event, the ministers were on the media. According to the immigration minister, Philip Ruddock, "a number" of children had been thrown overboard. "I regard this as one of the most disturbing practices I've come across," he said. "It was clearly planned and premeditated." The prime minister, John Howard, followed up in radio interviews over the next few days. "It doesn't speak volumes for some of the people on the vessel—suggestions that children were thrown overboard," he told one interviewer, and continued:

> It's not within my frame of comprehension that people who are genuine refugees would throw their people into the seas. I don't

want in this country people who are prepared, if those reports are true, to throw their children overboard. And that kind of emotional blackmail is very distressing … but we cannot allow ourselves to be intimidated by this.

Then journalists began asking for evidence. Questioned two days after the incident, the prime minister said that he'd been "acting on advice given to me by the immigration minister" to whom he had spoken shortly before he made the statement. "The advice I had," he continued,

> was that he had been informed they were thrown overboard and there were lifejackets … I can't tell you how many … As to the question of evidence … I'll make some inquiries and see what evidence can be made available … I have been provided with no information since then that would cause me to doubt it.

A few hours later, to confirm the account, the defence minister, Peter Reith, released two pictures of children in life jackets in the water with adults. They confirmed, he claimed, the horror of the event. In an election campaign being fought in a climate of fear following the terrorist attacks on 11 September and the arrival of the *Tampa*, here was the issue that could justify the government's position and help to keep it in office. "The fact," said Reith, "is that children were thrown into the water." He went on:

> I have subsequently been told they have also got film. The film is apparently on HMAS *Adelaide*. I have not seen it myself and apparently the quality of it is not very good and it's infra-red or something but I am told that someone has looked at it and it is an absolute fact, children were thrown into the water.

The publicity given to the event on the front pages of all the metropolitan newspapers set the tone for the campaign; the government would decide who came to this country.

Then, as suddenly as the event had hit the headlines, it died. After 14 October the incident barely rated a mention in the press for the next four weeks. But in election week it surfaced again. The *Australian* suggested the incident might not have happened; it cited reports of sailors on Christmas Island denying that any child had been thrown into the sea. Not so, insisted the prime minister at the National Press Club lunch, and he quoted a report from the intelligence agency, the Office of National Assessments, to back his case. He also released the video film of the events, and commented:

> [W]ell, in my mind there is no uncertainty because I don't disbelieve advice I was given by Defence ... I wasn't there, neither of the ministers were there. They get advice, it is then confirmed in writing in the terms I have described. I think in those circumstances it's perfectly reasonable and legitimate of me to say what I have said and I don't disbelieve the Defence advice.

As far as the government was concerned, it remained "an absolute fact".

Then followed a flurry of activity after the chief of the navy, Admiral Shackleton, gave a dockside interview as he left the *Adelaide*. The navy had advised the government that refugees had *threatened* to throw children overboard, he said, but he did not know what had happened to the message later. His statement appeared to contradict the government. A few hours later Shackleton issued a "clarifying" statement; he said starkly that the government had been advised that children were thrown overboard. The government won a sweeping victory two days later.

But the story was not true. No children were thrown overboard. The photographs published to verify the incident were taken later, when the ship was sinking and the refugees had entered the water at the request of the captain of the Australian naval vessel, the *Adelaide*, as it rescued them. Some of the figures in the water were Australian sailors who had dived in to assist the refugees. Within three days of the initial statements, the story was known to be untrue, by the crew of the *Adelaide*, by all but the very top level of the defence department. They knew, too, that the photographs did not support the story. Nor did a video of the events. Nor did a single written report from the *Adelaide*. There was never any evidence to sustain the story.

But the Australian people were not told it was false; no correction was made public before the election. Indeed the story was continually presented as "absolute fact", in Peter Reith's words.

How could that happen? How could an untrue story that was known to be untrue be sustained for so long? Who knew it was untrue and who did they tell? It was not as though this was an incident hidden in the inside sections of newspapers. It covered the front pages and was the first major story of the election, a story that set the tone for the campaign and gave the government the momentum it desired.

There is no difficulty now in determining the basic facts. No children were thrown overboard. The photographs—purportedly showing the incident—were taken a day later, after the story had become public. The video did not provide any evidence.

To recount and assess these events is not to suggest that the story changed the election result. But it surely helped to give the government an initiative and momentum that it never lost. The prime minister was probably going to win on the basis of his general approach to asylum seekers and as a consequence of the insecurity caused by 11 September. Indeed, the doubts in the last week about the veracity of the story may even have reduced the size of the victory. Nor am I concerned about whether, on other occasions, there may have been threats to throw children overboard, as government members of the Senate Select Committee on a Certain Maritime Incident (as it was formally known) suggested. This book is not about the behaviour of refugees, but about the shortcomings of Australian government.

The event was important for what it tells us about our political system, about the strains under which it works and its occasional failings. That is what this book is about: what happened, why it happened, and whether it should make us concerned about our political system. They are fundamental questions. Let us start with a basic proposition: *The Australian public was told a story that was untrue. That story was not corrected before the election, even though a wide range of people in and around the government knew it was untrue. If everyone acted properly and professionally, and we were still not told, something is seriously wrong with our system of government.* Unless we seek to learn from the experience, the problems will remain unidentified and unchanged.

What are the questions raised by the children overboard affair? The fundamental question is one of accountability. If someone—minister, officer or official—knows that a story being told in public is untrue, particularly a story that may have an impact on the outcome of an election, who has the responsibility to ensure that the public knows it is untrue?

Other questions emerge from that basic query. Are ministers "informed" if they are given a heavily qualified warning, or must it be explicit and in writing before they regard themselves as being advised? Can they choose not be informed, so that they have a level of "deniability" and can plead innocence?

Are ministerial staff still regarded as an extension of the minister, so that informing the staffer is considered to be the same as informing the minister? Or has the complexity of government, the increase in the number of staffers and the role that they now play long superseded so simple a concept—even if, in theory, they are still accountable only to the minister and not to parliament or the public? Can or should ministerial staffers give instructions to officials? Are they, as some regard themselves, the public servants' "bosses"? Are media advisers playing an ever-increasing role as they seek to "spin" the story to their minister's benefit and demand information constantly and immediately to feed the voracious demands of the daily media cycle?

The election campaign continued as these events unfolded. Did the caretaker conventions influence the way officials reacted? Does an election period make it harder for officials to judge what is partisan and what is not? Is it even harder when the polls suggest that the incumbent government is likely to be returned and the future of the public servants will be in the hands of the ministers they serve while the election is on?

How strongly should the officials of the public service, whether they are in the Department of Prime Minister and Cabinet, Defence, or Immigration, insist that ministers acknowledge advice, even if that advice is unwelcome? Has the Australian public service been made more craven or cautious by employment contracts or by the sacking of a number of departmental secretaries?

These events have been investigated by several inquiries. Directly after the election there were two reports by internal officers. A routine defence inquiry was undertaken by Major General Powell. From within the prime minister's department, assistant secretary Jennifer Bryant was commissioned by the departmental secretary, Max Moore-Wilton, at the request of the prime minister, to report on the events surrounding the whole advisory process. The Senate estimates committee took a first cut at a parliamentary investigation in February; then a Senate select committee examined the case in detail. Does the performance of the two parliamentary committees suggest that the parliament is able to investigate such events dispassionately, or are committees no more than another arena for party politics?

Each of these questions is significant for our system of government. We assume that the system works, at least adequately. Citizens may be sceptical about the behaviour of politicians, but they give high approval ratings to political institutions. This case suggests that some comfortable assumptions about our political institutions should be challenged. If the systems of accountability do not work, if there are flaws in different parts of the process, do we merely shrug and accept the shortcomings, or do we seek to amend the way they work?

But that is to jump ahead. First we need to set the scene, to construct as best we can an account of what happened, and of who knew what and how they reacted. Then we can go back to the principles of government and ask about their effectiveness.

This account is based on the hundreds of pages of transcript and evidence given to the internal inquiries and Senate committees. As well as telling us what happened, this material suggests explanations and motivations. Because some of the events are remembered differently by different participants, there will always be a degree of uncertainty at the edges. But not at the core.

CHAPTER 2
Behind the scenes

In October 2001 a substantial part of the Australian navy was patrolling the waters to our north and around the Australian dependency of Christmas Island. Its instructions were to detect, intercept, and turn back boats bringing unauthorised refugees. The *Tampa* incident had seen a massive switch in the government's standing; in that case, refugees from a sinking boat had been rescued by the Norwegian ship which then decided to land them on Christmas Island. The government refused to allow the refugees rescued by the *Tampa* to be landed on Australian soil. After a few days' stand-off, the government had come up with the "Pacific solution", under which it paid island countries to act as hosts while the status of the refugees was determined. It was expensive—Australia still paid the bills—but it maintained the policy of refusing to let them land. The government's popularity soared, and "border protection" was set as a primary issue for the forthcoming election.

Next, the government launched Operation Relex, designed to continue its strategy using the navy as a bulwark against invasion by leaky Indonesian vessels full of asylum seekers. The government's emotive term for the movement of asylum seekers was "people smuggling". Once the refugees had landed on

Australian shores they had a number of legal rights, so the government did not want them to land. The result was a constant game of cat and mouse between the navy and the refugee boats.

On 6 October the HMAS *Adelaide* was shadowing a boat designated SIEV4 (suspected illegal entry vessel 4), with 223 asylum seekers (SUNCs, in naval parlance) aboard, as it approached Australian territorial waters around Christmas Island. In the early hours of 7 October, having managed to slow down the vessel by firing across its bows, the *Adelaide* dispatched boarding parties in inflatable vessels. The boat stopped, its engine sabotaged. When the *Adelaide* approached, a number of the refugees jumped overboard. The *Adelaide*'s rescue boats pulled them out of the water and put them back on board. During that episode one refugee placed a life jacket on a small child in a yellow suit and walked to the edge of the boat, holding the child over the side. The crew of one of the inflatable boats told him to pull back, and he did so. The official moment-by-moment record of this incident, noted on the electrical optical tracking system, was as follows:

> 0558:52 MALE SUNC [suspected unauthorised non-citizen] ON UPPERDECK RETRIEVES SMALL CHILD (DAUGHTER WEARING A LIFE JACKET) FROM THE WHEELHOUSE
> 0600: MALE SUNC AND DAUGHTER AT GUARDRAIL STARBOARD SIDE UPPERDECK
> 0603:46 MALE SUNC GESTURES TO ADELAIDE PERSONNEL IN RHIB [inflatable vessel] LOCATED DIRECTLY BELOW HIM THAT HE WILL THROW HIS DAUGHTER OVER THE SIDE
> 0604:O5 MALE SUNC PLACES RIGHT LEG OVER THE UPPERDECK GUARDRAIL
> 0604:14 MALE SUNC AND DAUGHTER JOINED BY TWO OTHER MALE SUNCS

0604:41 MALE SUNC AND DAUGHTER MOVES BACK INBOARD
0604:41 TWO MEMBERS OF BOARDING PARTY MOVE IN BETWEEN MALE WITH DAUGHTER AND GUARDRAIL
0605:04 MALE SUNC WITH DAUGHTER MOVES BACK INBOARD

The whole incident took about 65 seconds. It was not recorded in any of the situation reports that the *Adelaide* sent to base because it was not seen as significant.

The Adelaide's technicians got the engine operating again, pointed the ship away from Australian shores, and sent the refugees on their way. It had been a tense situation, but well contained. When at sea the navy always has a primary responsibility to save lives that may be in danger; that responsibility is established by international convention and was, of course, the reason that the captain of the Tampa had intervened to rescue the earlier boatload of refugees. Given a choice between saving life and ensuring the refugees are kept away from Australia, the law of the sea gives priority to the former. In this case, all the people were rescued and the ship turned around; the Adelaide had fulfilled its responsibilities.

While these events were taking place, the captain of the *Adelaide*, Commander Norman Banks, received a phone call from his superior, Brigadier Silverstone, who was based in Darwin. Because these were sensitive operations, with instructions on actions against SIEVs sent through the chain of command, it was always necessary to keep up to date with what was happening. But this call was different. The minister for defence was to appear on a Sunday current affairs program, and needed to be briefed on recent developments. Silverstone had been instructed to ring the captain of the *Adelaide* and then tell the head of strategic command what was happening—a procedure that was not part of the normal chain of command. The head of strategic command was to brief the high-level taskforce established to monitor and advise on Operation Relex and then the minister.

The timing of the call was, perhaps, unfortunate. In his discussion with Silverstone, which took place while he was overseeing a dangerous and often fraught operation, Banks described what he saw. As best he can recall, he noted that one person was holding a child in a life jacket and was threatening to throw her overboard. He states that he did not say at any time that a child had been thrown overboard. Nor does the officer on the bridge with him during the phone conversation recall him saying a child had gone overboard. Silverstone gives the impression that during the call Banks seemed distracted, wanting to get off the phone and on with the job. Banks notes that "the telephone was used excessively by all parties (me included) for its convenience and guaranteed directness to the party concerned; however in the heat of the moment I often felt unnecessarily distracted by phone calls".

Distracted certainly, but not stressed. When it was suggested later that a misunderstanding could have occurred because of the "fog of war", Banks disagreed. The situation was not as serious as that phrase implies, and the *Adelaide* was at all times in reasonable control of the incident. He recalled later:

> The fog of war ... is a term that I did not introduce ... It is their expression, not mine. I view the events of 7 October and 8 October took place [*sic*] in a largely benign environment. The fog of war related more to a threat to the ship or to people. There was no threat to HMAS Adelaide or our people during the event. While I was concerned—and certainly during the hours of

darkness—at dawn, when the men overboard incidents took place, up until then I was fairly relaxed that we had effected a boarding safely and we were in control of the situation ... So I do not think the fog of war applies.

Silverstone took notes during the conversation. His notes record "men overboard", and after the phone was put down he added the word "child" between the two. He wrote "five, six or seven", an indication of the age that Banks thought the child might be. Silverstone has consistently been adamant that Banks said a child had been thrown overboard, and relied on his notes as evidence. Banks was initially unsure, particularly when faced by a senior officer who had taken notes at the time while he, Banks, was mid-operation and overseeing the crew. But as he reflected, and with the support of the officer on the bridge with him at the time, he became more certain that he did not say a child had been thrown overboard. The officer on the *Adelaide* said he heard Banks tell Silverstone "that the SUNCs are throwing themselves overboard and threatening to throw a child in the water in an attempt to create a SOLAS [safety of life at sea] situation". In retrospect, Banks suspected that "somewhere in the chain of command" statements about asylum seekers threatening to throw children overboard "were changed in translation" or "alternatively there was a political imperative and it was a deliberate change of the words signalled by the ship".

Precisely what was said in that call will never be known. Each participant sticks to his own version. But that conversation is the only source for the story that a child was thrown overboard. None of the situation reports sent by the *Adelaide* describing the events of 7 October made any mention of children being thrown or dropped into the water.

After speaking to Banks, Silverstone rang the head of strategic high command in Canberra, Air Vice Marshall Titheridge, and recounted what was happening on the *Adelaide*. It is not certain whether he said that a child or children had been thrown overboard. But the threat reported to Silverstone had now become a fact. Silverstone also rang his superior, Vice Admiral Smith, and gave the same report. Smith did not usually advise ministers directly, but that day he was in the company of the parliamentary secretary for defence, Brendan Nelson, and, when asked, told him that events had been made "much more difficult … by people jumping/ pushing people into the water". Smith thought Silverstone used the word children, rather than child.

In turn, Titheridge rang the defence minister's chief of staff. That, after all, had been the purpose of the initial call: to brief the minister. He also rang the chief of the defence force, Admiral Barrie, and the head of the people smuggling taskforce, Jane Halton, a deputy secretary in the prime minister's department. He told her that SUNCs had jumped overboard and that children were being thrown overboard, and insists that he would not have used the term "children" if Silverstone had not used the plural too. Halton asked him if they were all men, and recalls being told "we didn't think any women had gone in". She was interested in this point because "we all know that most of these women wear the hajib or something of that sort … and the notion of ending up in the water wearing a full hajib caused me some worry". Halton made her own note: "throwing kids o/b & trying to disable steering." She says she was told "children", not "child".

That call to Halton was to be the next vital link. With representatives from Immigration, Defence, and Foreign Affairs, the taskforce had been convened to coordinate the government's responses to the boats approaching Australia. Knowing that SIEV4 was arriving, and aware that the refugees were wearing lifejackets, the taskforce had convened that morning, even though it was a Sunday, to consider what responses were needed. As soon as it met, it was told that the refugees on SIEV4 were throwing children overboard. Exactly who told the taskforce is still uncertain; the Defence representative that morning, Group Captain Walker, has claimed it was not him, and indeed noted that he was embarrassed that Halton seemed to know more about events than he did. It seems probable that Halton, as chair of the taskforce, relayed the message she had just received from Titheridge. It was her practice to pass on verbatim messages from members of the taskforce unable to attend a meeting.

The secretary of the immigration department, Bill Farmer, was a member of the taskforce. During the meeting he received a call from his minister on his mobile phone. Ruddock was at a meeting of ethnic groups in Sydney; he knew that SIEV4 had been sighted, and wanted an up-to-date report before he went into the meeting. Farmer told him there were three distinctive features about this SIEV: the asylum seekers were wearing lifejackets, they were jumping overboard, and they were throwing children overboard. Farmer recalls:

> I told him [Ruddock] I was in the high-level group. I stayed at the table in the high-level group, and I made clear to him that I was doing that because I wanted to make sure that the information I was giving him was properly understood by me and by members of the group.

The taskforce considered how the news should be presented; its minutes noted: "Media lines were considered and provided to Mr Ruddock." The minister said nothing during his meeting, but as he left he held a media conference on the doorstop. He told journalists that refugees were throwing children overboard, and condemned these actions. He also rang the prime minister and the defence minister. On the afternoon after the taskforce had dispersed, Halton rang the prime minister's international affairs adviser, Miles Jordana, and the head of the prime minister's department, Max Moore-Wilton, to brief them on the developments.

Between Silverstone's call to Banks, when the refugees were being pulled out of the water, to the announcement by the minister no more than four hours had elapsed: a case of modern communications at their most effective. The story was out. Children (not *a* child, not a *threat*) were being thrown overboard by these heartless refugees.

At this stage every communication had been over the phone; there was no written advice.

With the story in the public domain, the next requirement was for evidence. What took place, in effect, were two searches based on different frames of reference. Defence began to check for evidence for the original account. This search followed standard practice—after all, it is not unusual for reports given in the rush of events to be found to be inaccurate. As Group Captain Walker commented later:

> In my experience … the first report of any incident is usually wrong. However ministerial staff and other departments will press for immediate detail. The former can be mitigated by dwelling a pause and by trusting documented rather than verbal reports, but this process increases the time factor. Give people sufficient authority/ top cover to hold the wolves at bay until the picture is accurately known. Education, experience, courage and tact are required to achieve this aim.

So Walker went to look for a clear account of what had happened.

Others had a different agenda. Ministerial staff wanted more information to drive home the impression already presented to the public. They wanted details, pictures, anything for the follow-up stories. The members of the taskforce wanted evidence, too, working on the assumption that the initial story was true.

The defence minister's media adviser, Ross Hampton, quickly rang the watchkeeper for Strategic Command, Flight Lieutenant Jason Briggs. According to the Bryant report:

> Flight Lieutenant Briggs stated that Mr Hampton asked him if there was information on children being thrown into the water. Flight Lieutenant Briggs informed him that there wasn't. Soon after that Group Captain Walker had returned from the IDC [taskforce] meeting and asked the same question. After going back through all the written material, Flight Lieutenant Briggs rang AST [Australian theatre command] and asked if they had any information on this incident and they said that they didn't. Flight Lieutenant Briggs said he started compiling the faxes for Ross Hampton and the faxes sent to Mr Hampton were essentially paraphrasing the situation reports from HMAS Adelaide. Each fax was sent in response to one or more calls from Mr Hampton.

When Briggs told his superior that, since the signals from *Adelaide* were all "ops normal", there was no point sending them on, he was told to "put everything that came in into a fax for Mr Hampton". On this day Hampton seemed to defence officers to be "agitated and quite angry at times, saying that he was under pressure from media outlets to meet their publication deadlines. He was concerned about the lack of precise information". What for Hampton was a lack of detail was for Walker a reason for questioning the original story.

The taskforce met again on the evening of 7 October to consider a paper, "Options for Handling Unauthorised Arrivals: Christmas Island Boat", written that day for presentation to the prime minister. It included a statement that the *Adelaide*'s attempt to return the ship to international waters "has been met with attempts to disable the vessel, passengers jumping into the sea and passengers throwing their children into the sea". Walker mentioned that there was no evidence to substantiate the story. He said later that when he had gone back to headquarters to try to confirm this information he found "nothing in the written message traffic that mentioned children". At the evening meeting of the taskforce he pointed out that he had no written confirmation that children had gone into the water:

> That was not to say it did not happen, but what I was trying to stress was that I had no auditable evidence that children had gone into the water. Since I did not know what the source of the information was—that is, where Ms Halton had got the information—basically I was trying to say to her, "Since I can't prove what you're saying, I think you should go back and check from your source that you are happy the information is correct".

Walker's comments led to a discussion about who had told the taskforce in the first place. The secretary of the immigration department thought it was Defence; Walker denied it. Most of the others thought it had been Halton.

Members of the taskforce noted that the paper also contained a number of statements accompanied by caveats. For instance, the paper gave an estimate of the number of SUNCs on the boat, but with the caution that the number might have to be revised. There was no such caveat after the sentence on children thrown overboard, so the taskforce members took it as given. Titheridge said later that if he had made the initial report to the taskforce he would have added a caveat because of the nature of the information. By this stage Titheridge had replaced Walker as the defence representative, and he did not question the story he had passed on that morning. There was no change to the original text. The comment remained in the paper; the story was set. It was approved and sent to the prime minister and other ministers. Here was the original—and, as it turned out, the only—written advice. The basic proposition was that it had happened. If anyone wanted it to be denied they had to prove it did not happen, and proving a negative is hard.

How did this happen? General Powell's report attributed it to "a combination of haste, over-enthusiasm, errors of judgement, misunderstanding and misinterpretation". But, he went on,

> ultimately it was a direct result of the conflicting balance between the provision of timely information versus accurate information ... Information should be corroborated at each level of command. Where shortcuts are taken to meet demanding timeframes, there is a significant risk of inaccurate information being provided.

News moved faster than any corroboration. Ministers did not wish to wait; nor did the senior public servants ask for a check to be made. As Banks recalled, "The 'alleged' recollection of phone conversations were at variance to my signalled summaries at the time". But no one challenged that difference. "No one called back to question me on what I had or had not seen."

As part of the routine procedure, one signal was sent early on the Monday morning to the prime minister's department and the prime minister's office. It stated that men had gone overboard. It made no mention of children. It was based on the signals from *Adelaide*.

On 8 October the children overboard story was on the front page of every newspaper. The refugees were demonised as heartless. The government had grabbed its opportunity.

Meanwhile, at sea, SIEV4 was in more trouble. The *Adelaide* had shadowed it overnight, and in the early hours the engine had stopped and the refugees had raised a distress signal. Deciding that the situation had changed, that the *Adelaide* was now responsible for saving lives at sea, the naval vessel took the boat in tow. Then, whether from sabotage or as a consequence of being towed, SIEV4 began to sink. Dispatching rescue boats and rafts to assist, Commander Banks instructed that some of the refugees get into the water to make rescue easier. Seven of his crew dived in to assist by holding up the women and children in their life jackets until the boats arrived. The rescue took some hours. The sailors in the water with the refugees were photographed, as were the sinking boat and the refugees on board the *Adelaide*. Proud of his crew, the captain sent a selection of the pictures on the secure email to a list of people in Defence. All the refugees were rescued before the vessel finally sank. No life was lost.

On the same day the chief of the defence force, Admiral Barrie, talked to Peter Reith and to Max Moore-Wilton. Moore-Wilton wanted to make sure that all the refugees would be picked up by the *Adelaide*; he wanted none of them to be rescued by boats from Christmas Island and landed there. Barrie told both men that, if the refugees were at risk, the first priority of the *Adelaide* must be to ensure no lives were lost; what happened afterwards could be sorted out later.

On 9 October a reporter from Channel 10 managed to get through to the captain of the *Adelaide*. Banks was somewhat surprised by the call, which dragged him out of the shower. Although it was strictly forbidden, he answered a number of questions. He refused to talk about any policy or operational issues but, not unreasonably, was delighted to tell the reporter what a great job his crew had done in rescuing the refugees, and about the care and consideration with which they had treated them. He revealed that a number of photos had been taken of the rescue.

The interview was innocuous; as Vice Admiral Ritchie's own jottings, given to the select committee, note: "Banks talks to press—no relevant detail is passed." But the captain was strongly counselled against doing it again. He gave a detailed account of what was said, and noted later that he was "now fully aware of the political ramifications/ sensitivities of this operation and will ensure that no further media questions are answered".

According to regulations promulgated by the secretary of defence and the chief of the defence force, at the instruction of the minister, all communications with the media were to go through official channels. For Operation Relex the rules were even tighter: all requests for information had to go the media adviser to the defence minister. The head of the defence department's public affairs division was furious about Banks's interview with Channel 10. She demanded that the minister's media adviser be told and assured it would not happen again, and that the circumstances be investigated.

Banks later "actively encouraged the ship's company to avoid discussing the incidents outside official channels". But when the harbour master of Christmas Island came aboard, he and Banks discussed the recent events; neither was happy with the way the facts had been twisted. As they talked about the media coverage, according to Banks, the harbour master "indicated that this whole show was wrong (and I agreed with him),

"Nosedive" (top) and "Swimming", two of
the photographs taken—along with the better-known
"Laura the hero"—on 8 October, the day after the
alleged children overboard incident

and we spoke of how political this whole event was becoming"

> I showed him footage of the sinking and the boarding, including the man overboard incidents—principally because it was scattered around my cabin as I was preparing the post incident statements etc. I also mentioned that to our knowledge media reporting of the incident to date had been inaccurate—he agreed.

Banks felt that stories from Christmas Island reported later in the *Australian* may have originated in this conversation aboard the *Adelaide*.

Questions were already beginning to be asked, however. Media reports claimed that after SIEV4 had been halted men had jumped overboard as a result of shots being fired at the boat. At a meeting of the taskforce Halton was concerned by the story, and told the defence representative "that they had better be certain about the veracity of the initial reports and they should do some searching". The prime minister's office was asking for additional details. The taskforce was also annoyed by the interview Banks had given to Channel 10, and demanded the provision of more timely information. This may have been the meeting at which, according to the recollection of another delegate, Admiral Bonser, a debate took place about whether the incident had happened. The prime minister's office was told that the taskforce had requested corroborative evidence.

But the principal cat Banks had let loose was the mention of photographs of the incident. Channel 10 rang the Department of Defence to ask for pictures of the *Adelaide*, the captain, and the incident. The defence minister's media adviser immediately asked for copies of the photos.

Attached to the photos were titles and captions. The titles were brief; the captions consisted of a longer explanatory text and the date on which the photo was taken. Thus the title of one of the two photos released soon after was "Laura the hero" (which appears on the cover of this book). The caption read:

> ABBM Laura Whittle was recently photographed as the navy Value "Courage". During the 08 Oct rescue of 223 SUNCs from a sinking Indonesian fishing vessel, Able Seaman Whittle again typified this true quality through her immense courage in leaping 12 metres from the ship's 02 deck into the water to drag women and children to the safety of a liferaft. Selflessly she entered the water without a lifejacket and without regard for her own safety to help others in need.

There was some difficulty at first in getting access to the photos. The *Adelaide* had sent them by secret email to several addresses in Defence, and some parts of the department were not able to print them out when they were transferred from the "secret" to "restricted" systems. When Hampton demanded copies be sent over, the person instructed to send them created a new email, without captions, containing two pictures of people in the water. Who decided not to include the captions, or whether it was an accident, is a matter of dispute. The officer who initially sent the photos was not aware that captions existed. Whatever the explanation, their omission led to immediate misunderstandings. Did the photos show the children overboard incident that everyone was talking about? Or did they show the sinking of the vessel a day later? Hampton later commented that "during the time the photos were released everyone was talking about the children overboard incident—no one was talking about the sinking". He assumed the photos related to the incident. The Defence media liaison officer believed they were connected with the Banks interview and the sinking. Besides, Defence already had other pictures that portrayed the sinking.

The same day, amid growing doubts about whether any children had indeed been thrown overboard, Defence's checks escalated. Both of Banks's superiors up the chain of command, Brigadier Silverstone and Rear Admiral Smith, had noted that none of the signal traffic from *Adelaide* had made any mention of the incident. Smith rang Banks direct to discuss what had happened. By the end of the call he had doubts that any children had gone overboard, and he passed those doubts on to Admiral Ritchie. Silverstone instructed the captain of the *Adelaide* to collect sworn statements from crew involved with SIEV4 on 7 October to determine precisely what had happened that day. There were now two sets of questions: had children been thrown overboard, and which events were shown in the photos?

The first question was settled, at least within Defence, the next day. At noon on 10 October the captain of the *Adelaide* reported to his superiors that no children had been thrown overboard. Four hours later, sixteen statutory statements from the crew of the *Adelaide* were forwarded through the chain of command. None of them said they had seen children thrown overboard, although one thought he might have seen one child jump. They did recall a child in a lifejacket being held over the side and then being pulled back. The crew was well aware of the way the events were being interpreted in the media; they wondered how the story had been created, and were annoyed that their actions were being misrepresented. Banks seems to have been conscious of problems ahead: when he sent the written summary and the crew's statements to Silverstone, he asked, "Should I seek legal advice as I feel the wolves circling?" But he was directed explicitly that it was not his role to remedy the "misinterpretation". Later that day he sent his own statement to Silverstone denying that he had ever said a child had been thrown overboard. In other words, by 10 October he had no doubts.

Based on the statements of the crew, Silverstone duly sent an email to his superiors at 1.15 pm on 11 October:

> Until 10 Oct CO ADE [Commanding Officer, Adelaide] believed that the reports of the disposal of a child overboard remained credible. In a later conversation with me on Tue he reported that this now did not appear to be the case. I believe there is ample reporting here, pending CO ADE's statement, that there was a great deal of confusion, that the adult SUNCs were intent on provoking an incident and that a report of a child deliberately placed overboard was credible at that time. It is only some days later when that perception was tested that it became clear that no one recovered any children from the water ... At this point I can only conclude, pending CO ADE's statement, that he believed at the time in the confusion of events that a child was disposed of overboard and reported in good faith.

To suggest a report was "credible at that time" implies it no longer is, and that it should be corrected.

In his later statement Banks denied he had said a child had been thrown overboard. He claimed to have stated that he saw a man threatening to put a child over the side. He stuck to that story. But whichever account was true, Silverstone's superiors up to the level below the chief of defence force, Rear Admirals Smith and Ritchie, now knew that no children had been tossed into the sea. Defence with a capital D, as Barrie described himself to the Senate estimates committee, was informed by the afternoon of 10 October when Ritchie told the chief of the defence force of the doubts.

During the day, in response to the request from the taskforce for evidence, a chronology of events developed by strategic command was sent to the Department of Prime Minister and Cabinet. Four dot points, later called footnotes, came at the end of the chronology. Two described the boat; one guessed at the number of refugees aboard. The fourth footnote stated: "There is no indication that children were thrown overboard. It is possible that this did occur in conjunction with other SUNCs jumping overboard." Walker commented:

> Again, that was, from my perspective, to say, "On Sunday evening, I had asked you to go back and check your sources". Once again, it was a reminder, "Would you check your sources?" because I did not know and I still do not know where that information came from.

According to Titheridge, the chronology was also sent to the minister's defence adviser, Mike Scrafton.

But the warning was not heeded. Halton had been interstate for the day, and arrived back at the department at 4.45 pm, just in time to chair another meeting of the taskforce. On the way to her office, she met Katrina Edwards, secretary to the taskforce, who told her that strategic command had reported there was "no documentary evidence of children thrown overboard". In her office Halton rang the minister's chief of staff and Titheridge. She also took a call from the minister, Peter Reith, who told her that there were photos, statements, and a video to back up the story. She went to the taskforce meeting satisfied that here was the confirmation the taskforce had been seeking. Edwards thought that the "follow-up occurred at the expense of my being able to brief Ms Halton effectively on the other substantial developments of the day". The chronology was never given to the taskforce, but the prime minister's department had been alerted to strategic command's conclusion, and Edwards had sought to draw Halton's attention to it. Halton chased up the existence of the video and finally confirmed its existence from Scrafton. She updated Jordana and Moore-Wilton. Then, for her, the issue was "at rest". That day, 10 October, was the last time the taskforce dealt with SIEV4.

Halton had asked for the evidence from Defence, demanding they check their facts. Why not pay attention, then, to their report? She explained:

> That footnote appeared as a footnote on a fax to a junior officer in PM&C [Department of Prime Minister and Cabinet] and was not accompanied by a phone call to me or anybody else to say, "Actually, we are a bit concerned now that there is a doubt here". We were never told there was doubt … If you have a concern, you pick up a phone and ring me … [O]nly a footnote and it was not accompanied by a red light flashing and a warning bell.

The information did not flow up, the officials in the prime minister's department noted, because when the photos were released later that day they thought the question had been resolved. Edwards explained: "We had been basically assured that the incident had happened and that there was a body of evidence to support it. As I said, the photos appeared, so there no reason to pursue the inquiries any further." As Halton had been told by the minister and his officers, there were photos, statements from the crew, and a video; she and her colleagues were not to know yet that none of these sources provided the positive evidence that they were assured was there.

Much of the activity that day related to the release of the photos. In the morning a member of the prime minister's staff had rung Hampton to ask if there were photos that could be released to back up the story. Hampton demanded that copies be provided, and the defence liaison officer sent the two photos to the minister's office with titles but no text. The minister, Peter Reith, rang the chief of the defence force to ask if there were any operational or security reasons to prevent their release. Barrie had not seen the pictures, so he agreed to ask Titheridge, who contacted Reith five minutes later to say that there was no problem. Because several sets were doing the rounds in Defence, it is not clear which group of photographs was being discussed. Hampton instructed Defence public relations to release the photos to any media outlet that asked. To avoid identifying individual sailors the photos went out without captions or titles.

Hampton was still searching for good evidence. He asked a public relations officer how many children had gone overboard and whether there was any reason why the minister should not release that information. But a search could not find anything. The watchkeeper in strategic command was "puzzled by the media reports because he couldn't remember seeing the detail in the internal reporting". He told the inquiry:

> In the meantime Ross Hampton called again and was agitated because I did not have the information he wanted. When I advised that it was taking some time to answer his question because I could not find any reference to children being pushed overboard in any reporting, he became extremely agitated.

Hampton also asked to speak direct to the captain of the *Adelaide*, but Rear Admiral Smith did not approve. That was one channel too far.

Defence had been told that Reith would agree to release the

photos in a doorstop interview that afternoon, but they now realised the photos might be misrepresented. At 3.30 pm Brigadier Bornholt, attached to Defence's public affairs division, rang Hampton to suggest that the photos about to be released might not show the alleged children overboard incident. As Bornholt was looking at a set of five pictures of the sinking and Hampton at two of people in the water, they seemed to be talking at cross purposes. There is some dispute about which set of photos each of them had. Hampton later argued that the chief of the defence force had confirmed the pictures were of the incident—but he had not, as he had not seen them. Bornholt agreed to check, satisfied himself that they all related to the sinking, and left a message on the media adviser's answering machine. But Hampton never rang back. On radio, Reith referred to the photos and to a video of the events that he had not seen but had been told showed the children being thrown overboard. "It's an absolute fact," he emphasised.

The minister's senior adviser was also told on 10 October that the electrical optical tracking system video did not show any children being thrown into the water. Ritchie's statement said:

> On this day I recorded that Strategic Command has said no evidence of children thrown overboard ... the question was asked; Were they? I have then recorded that the Electro optical film shows no children being thrown overboard ... Told M Scrafton.

Indeed, he told Scrafton more than that. When Scrafton rang to ask him about evidence in support of the claim that children were thrown overboard, Ritchie told him of the doubts about whether the events had occurred at all.

When the photographs were broadcast on the ABC's *7.30 Report*, Defence immediately realised that they showed the

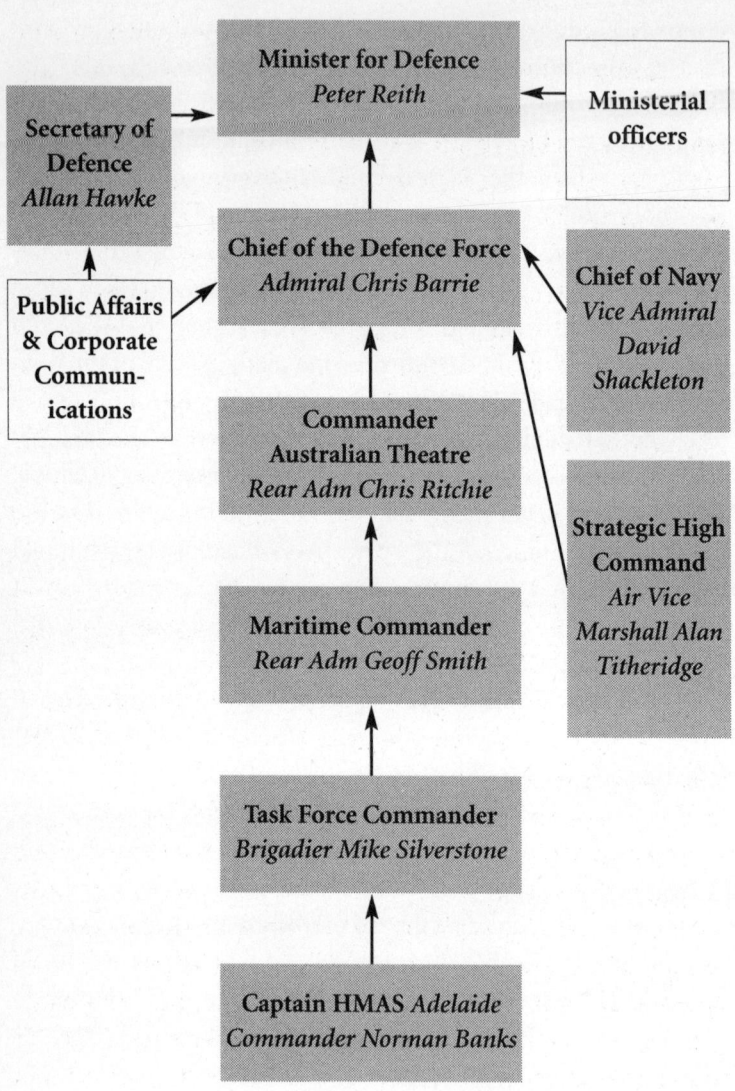

Defence chain of command, October 2001

wrong incident. Smith contacted Ritchie and the chief of navy, Rear Admiral Shackleton. Both of them told the chief of the defence force that the photos were of a different event. Scrafton, the minister's defence adviser, was also told that the videotape did not contain evidence to show that children had been thrown overboard. (The photos showed women and children in the water, yet the head of strategic command had told Halton that no women had gone overboard on 7 October. No one seemed to notice the discrepancy.) An immediate effort was made within Defence to correct the record.

The secretary of the department, Allan Hawke, had not played a major role so far because reports of what happened at sea were the responsibility of the chief of the defence force. Under the diarchy in Defence (see opposite) the secretary stays out of military operations. But once the department's public affairs division, the PACC, had become involved it was part of his responsibility. He told the head of public affairs to inform the minister in writing that the photos did not refer to the day when children were allegedly thrown overboard. The head, Jenny McKenry, and the defence officer attached to Defence public affairs, Brigadier Bornholt, talked to Mike Scrafton. But rather than provide that advice in writing as requested by the secretary of the department, McKenry acceded to Scrafton's request and only sent on an email containing a set of captioned pictures and, later, an explanation from the Defence media liaison officer of how the photos were sent to Hampton without captions. In other words, as the secretary of the department noted to the committee, "what Scrafton asked for was what Ms McKenry sent forward". Hawke agreed with the proposition that she had done what Scrafton had asked her to do "rather than what you, Dr Hawke, the secretary of the department, asked her to do". McKenry sent Hawke a copy of her email to Scrafton; he acknowledged it without asking for further action.

Hawke later publicly regretted his inaction. "I feel I could have done more on the issue," he told the committee, "by talking directly to the minister and providing him with clear written advice to that effect." Indeed he offered his resignation to the new minister for his failure to press the point and advise the minister about the misrepresentation of the photos. McKenry was also concerned that there were copies of the photos, with captions, on the restricted system, and they might be leaked to the press before the minister had time to correct the record. She ordered that they all be deleted, and waited for the correction.

Smith says that Ritchie told the chief of the defence force, Admiral Barrie, about the doubts. Although Ritchie has no precise memory of the conversation, he is "fairly confident" that he would have told Barrie. Barrie did talk to the minister that morning about the photos, and there were discussions within the minister's office about whether there should be a retraction of the claims made for the photographs—although neither the chief of the defence force nor the minister recall exactly what was said. Barrie recalls:

> The following day I had a telephone conversation with Minister Reith about photographs. I told him I had been advised that the photographs he had put out did not describe the events as he portrayed on the *7.30 Report*. I cannot remember his precise response, save that we had a discussion about there being a great deal of confusion about the photographs. But I do recall our conversation was testy. It concluded with an agreement between us that never again would we discuss photographs without ensuring that we both had the same photographs in front of us.

It was, as he put it, "a conversation in which I would say the ministers give directions and CDFs [chiefs of the defence force] give advice". But the conversation never went to the question of what might be done about it.

By more direct means Hampton also obtained another copy of the photos. He phoned a defence officer and, when he did not get immediate action, became insistent. "I am the boss of HPACC", he said, "and I am your boss." He refused to hang up until the photos had been emailed to him. This time the email included captions making it clear the photos showed the sinking of the vessel, not the earlier incident. Hampton's recollection to the Bryant inquiry is that the minister asked for a "formal response to these rumours because the matter is not yet resolved. At this time"—he was speaking in December 2001—"we have not yet received a conclusive reply to this matter from Defence." Defence cannot recall this request.

Clearly, by 11 October the defence minister's office knew the photos had been misleading. It was agreed, the chief of the defence force's staff understood, that the issue would be dropped. Barrie was also told on 11 October by Ritchie that there were now doubts about whether children were ever thrown overboard. Barrie told him that the photographs were only part of the evidentiary material, and that until he could produce evidence to show that the original report was wrong he would not change his advice to the minister. He demanded compelling evidence. "If my commanders are absolutely thoroughly convinced that I am wrong," he said, "I would expect them to come back and say 'CDF, you are wrong'. That never happened."

Barrie told the Senate estimates committee:

> It was my judgement that the commanding officer ought to be supported and his judgement ought to stand ... I was not per-

suaded that there was compelling evidence that the CO of Adelaide was wrong.

His stance is puzzling on two counts. It is at odds with his colleagues in Defence who, overwhelmingly, were sceptical about the initial reports, which they believed should be checked and confirmed. And he was disagreeing with the very officer—Banks—whom he claimed to be supporting. But he left it to his subordinates to come back with the evidence. They never tried to persuade him again. Despite earlier opportunities, he did not talk to Banks until after the estimates hearings in February.

What did the minister's office do after 11 October when it was told that the photos were wrong? Reith's chief of staff, Peter Hendy, said that "they never got a clear answer on whether or not the photos were from the sinking ..." He was, however, "100% certain that on the day of the release the office was told the photos were of the children overboard".

When the accuracy of the attribution of the photos was challenged, the minister made the decision within 24 hours that he would not change the public record until he had conclusive advice about the original reports and the photos. Media adviser Ross Hampton still argued to the Bryant inquiry in December that it was not clear to him that the photos weren't from 7 October. He couldn't remember whether the office discussed a retraction because "at that stage it was between the Minister, Mr Hendy and Mr Scrafton and that he couldn't comment on what consideration if any was given to a retraction". He argued that ministers should always work from written advice. The Bryant inquiry noted Scrafton said that:

> he was aware of some discussion about retraction, within the office (including between Mr Hampton and Mr Hendy). However

he noted that it was a political issue and that therefore Mr Scrafton was not involved in any decision making. Mr Scrafton said in his assessment, there was a judgement made that the photographs had been widely distributed on the Restricted system and were available to a large number of people. He considered that the political solution was "not to raise" the issue. He was not sure if Mr Reith had been party to these judgements.

The Bryant inquiry summarised the responses it had received from the minister:

> He and the office remained sceptical and uncertain that the photographs were not from the overboard incident. He stated that saying he had "made the decision not to change the public record" implied that he accepted the photographs had been misrepresented, whereas the reality was there was continuing uncertainty and he was not willing to make further public comments which may have themselves not have been correct.

Silence, leaving the original story alive, was the preferred tactic. As Scrafton said, it was the political choice. When Reith says he never received advice, he may not have been given written advice. Throughout this affair, what constitutes "advice" is significant.

The same day another channel was opened into the prime minister's department. The defence liaison officer in the international division, Commander Stefan King, was told by Defence that the photographs had been wrongly attributed. He passed on the information to his immediate superior, Harinder Sidhu. She thought it to be sufficiently perturbing that the assistant secretary of the division, Brendon Hammer, should be informed immediately. When talking to Sidhu and Hammer, King did not name his source. As far as he was concerned these were formal briefings in which he fulfilled his obligations to liaise, particularly because, as Hammer acknowledged, he had been asked to give him "briefings on Operation Relex". The officers in the prime minister's department do not seem to have understood the import of the information. Sidhu thought the information had been passed on over a cup of tea. Hammer regarded King as a defence secondee rather than as an official liaison officer. For Hammer this was "very low-grade low-quality information" from a junior officer, and he wondered why he was being bothered by such detail. He saw his job was to "prioritise". "I push aside, I filter out extraneous unreliable material," he said later. Nor, he believed, did this information come into his area of responsibility. He assumed that the taskforce, with its links higher in the defence forces, would hear if there were significant doubts. For these reasons he did not pass on the story. "You do not bother the Prime Minister or the secretary or a deputy secretary or whoever with material that just looks fishy," he told the select committee. The defence liaison officer was never told what was done with the information. And when, in November, the two parts of the prime minister's department connected and pooled their information, this formal briefing was treated by the international division officers as "tea room gossip", to use the prime minister's phrase.

After 11 October the issue suddenly disappears. Despite the fact that it seemed like a gift to ministers, they didn't choose to use it again. Why not? What governments choose *not* to talk about is as often as significant as what they choose to talk about. Election strategy is planned to the last phrase and intonation. A decision to drop a subject as evocative as children overboard would not be an accident or an oversight, it would be part of a deliberate political process. Perhaps in this case the knowledge that the photos misrepresented the case had spread. Better to move on and not admit it than to continue to talk of SIEV4 and risk having to reveal the truth. Perhaps there were other reasons. But the shift was abrupt. From that time on, the case was only raised by the media, never by the government.

On 17 October Barrie had another conversation with the minister.

> I informed him that I had been informed by the Chief of Navy and COMAST [Ritchie] that there were doubts about whether children had ever been thrown over the side of SIEV4. I said to him the doubts seemed to be based on what the photographs showed— or did not show—and an inconclusive video. I said that I had indicated to them my position was that, until evidence was produced to show the initial report to me was wrong I would stand by it.

He didn't change his advice. The equivocation was all the minister needed. When Reith was asked again on 17 October, he referred to the video. He had not seen it, it was grainy and infrared, but again it was an absolute fact that children had been thrown overboard. This was strange, as no one in Defence ever told him that the video showed children thrown overboard.

Defence suggested the issue simply disappeared off the radar, eclipsed by other pressing issues. As the chief of the defence force later told the select committee:

> We do have some very serious circumstances in front of us. We have a situation in the Middle East which, in my view, is out of control and which could easily lead to very serious consequences for us all ... I can tell you there are some key analysts in the United

States and there are analysts in this country who are forecasting a prospect of the third world war. These are serious times in that sense. I am not trying to underestimate the value of this committee's work in making us a better ADF—I am not trying to say that—but, in that sense, we have to concentrate on what is really important.

So it disappeared as an issue, and most of those who had been involved hoped it would stay that way. Although it did not resurface immediately, there were occasions when it might have. The prime minister visited the *Adelaide* on 24 October; he talked to the crew and asked some if they had been involved in the rescues. The crew had been advised in a group meeting that they were not to talk to the media and that they should only speak to the PM if asked direct questions. Howard discussed cricket with the captain. He praised them for their actions. But he never mentioned, and never asked about, the children overboard.

Another week later, during a visit to northern command on 31 October, Peter Reith asked Silverstone if he had seen the video. Silverstone notes he was amazed that the minister still stuck to the original, incorrect story and had not been advised otherwise. He told the minister "the video does not show a child being thrown into the water". According to Silverstone, the minister replied with words to the effect that, "well, we'd better not see the video then". He seems not to have taken the advice seriously, and continued to refer to the video as evidence—even though Ritchie believes that no one, to his knowledge, had ever told the minister that the video showed children being thrown overboard.

Then, in the week of the election, the *Australian* ran a story, based on accounts from the crew of the *Adelaide* when they were on Christmas Island, that no children had been thrown overboard. Reith wanted to discuss the article, so on 7 November the acting chief of the defence force, Air Vice Marshal Houston, looked at the available evidence—but not at the video, because there was no copy in Canberra. He then had a lengthy discussion with the chief of the defence force's staff and with Brigadier Bornholt. He was shown the message from the *Adelaide* of 10 October that decisively stated that no child had been thrown. With Bornholt listening in on a speaker phone, Houston rang the minister.

> I started off by telling him I felt that it had been a very confused situation but from the evidence that I had seen it appeared to me that there had been a boarding operation on the 7th, people had jumped into the water, there had been an incident with a child being held over the water, but fundamentally there was nothing to suggest that women and children had been thrown into the water …

He told him the video was inconclusive and that the photos related to the events of 8 October, not the previous day.

> After I had given him this run down of what happened there was silence for quite a while. It seemed to me he was stunned and surprised. Essentially he then said, "Well, I think we'll have to look at releasing the video".

Reith's defence adviser, Mike Scrafton, watched a copy of the video, which had now arrived. It seemed inconclusive. He talked to the prime minister a couple of times and told him it was inconclusive because it did not provide evidence of children being thrown overboard. The prime minister decided to release the video.

The next day, Howard was due to appear before the Press Club in Canberra, and the allegations in the *Australian* were bound to be raised by journalists. So his international adviser, Miles Jordana, started looking for more evidence. He rang the Department of Prime Minister and Cabinet, and asked for copies of the situation reports from the *Adelaide*. While the officers from the social policy division were looking for situation reports they heard additional stories from the international division that the photos had been misrepresented. Those reports were treated as "tearoom gossip", but they were more than that because the international division had been told three weeks before, through the defence liaison officer, that the photos had been misrepresented. Halton was duly advised, and says that she was "shocked" by the news. She rang Jordana to tell him. In a letter to Moore-Wilton in February she wrote:

> Mr Jordana's response was to the effect that, yes, there was already speculation in the press, they were on to it and they were talking to Mr Reith's office. Consistent with my practice of keeping you informed, I also believe that I rang you to pass this on but that from memory we did not speak and I left an voicemail message (I cannot be categorical on this point).

Jordana did not find the evidence from the *Adelaide* useful (which was not surprising, as it could scarcely report an incident that did not occur), so he went to other sources.

The Office of National Assessments (ONA) is the government's intelligence analysis organisation. On 9 October it had circulated a report on people smuggling which stated that when the *Adelaide* intercepted the SIEV4 "asylum seekers wearing lifejackets jumped into the sea and children were thrown in with them". It went on to suggest that these tactics had been used on other occasions—against the Italian navy, for example. Where did the evidence come from, the prime minister's office wanted to know? ONA at least put the answer in writing:

> Our report was published on 9 October, but a press report of 8 October quoted the PM referring to children being thrown into the water. So the PM's information must have come from a source other than the ONA report … we are not yet able to identify the source of the information in the ONA report though it could have been based on the Ministers' statements. But there may also have been Defence reporting for which we are searching.

As the ONA noted in a minute to the prime minister a week later, after the election, there was no defence reporting that suggested children were thrown overboard. Its report was based entirely on ministers' statements.

So there was not much left of the evidence that had been presented a month earlier. The photographs were of the wrong incident. The video showed no such event. The international affairs adviser in the prime minister's office knew that the ONA report was probably based on ministers' speeches, and therefore corroborated nothing. Yet on the evening of 7 November, when the prime minister talked to Reith, they were still treating the original story seriously. Both men say that Houston's advice was not mentioned during the conversation, Reith later saying he wanted to wait for advice from the chief of the defence force. Reith admitted there were doubts about the story but he had not been formally advised that the event had not happened.

At the Press Club lunch the prime minister vigorously defended the government. He argued that he "had acted in good faith" because he had been advised by the ONA that "asylum seekers ... were thrown into the water". So the prime minister was quoting the ONA which was quoting the prime minister:

> The whole basis of our claim was the advice we received[.] [N]ow if you get that kind of written advice and you get the sort of advice that Mr Ruddock and Mr Reith received at the time, that is the basis of the allegations that are made.
>
> I have to say to all of you who have raised queries about this, if a Defence Minister and an Immigration Minister get verbal advice from defence sources and then a prime minister gets that kind of written advice I don't think it is sort of exaggerating or gilding the lily to go out and say what I said.

At the same time Reith claimed that the "advice I had at the time and the statement that I made was that I received advice which said that the video confirmed the advice that I had". In all the parliamentary committee hearings no one could find anyone who gave that advice. The defence was now based not on evidence but on the fact that advice was given and that ministers should have the right to accept it.

On 9 November the chief of the navy, Admiral Shackleton, visited the *Adelaide* in Perth just before it was to leave for a tour of duty in the Persian Gulf. During the visit he discussed the SIEV4 incident with Commander Banks. When asked afterwards what had actually occurred on 7 October, he replied: "Our advice was that people were being threatened with being thrown in the water and I don't know what happened to the message after that." The comment created headlines; the navy seemed to be contradicting the government just a day before the election.

The reaction from Canberra was rapid. Shackleton was rung by the head of the minister's office to ask what his statement implied. The secretary of the defence department was contacted by the secretaries of the immigration department and the prime minister's department to discover what had been meant by the statement. He asked the head of Defence public affairs to assist in drawing up a clarifying statement, which Shackleton agreed to issue. He denied he had contradicted the government. "I confirm", the statement went on, "the minister was advised that Defence believed children had been thrown overboard". Succinct and accurate, the statement left open the possibility that the incident may not have happened.

Howard had already recorded one interview for that evening's edition of the ABC program, *Lateline*. At his request a second was undertaken so that he could defend the government.

> The reason I wanted to clarify this is that I reject any suggestion that we made up this story. Mr Reith would never have made those comments, Mr Ruddock would have never made them, I would have never made them if we hadn't received advice to that effect.

"If in fact what Mr Reith and Mr Ruddock said a month ago was wrong", he added, "I think it would have been a good idea if they had been told." In at least one case they were, even if they did not want to know and chose to await further advice.

Before the story could unfold any further, the government was returned with a convincing victory, but the imbroglio of the last week had raised a number of questions.

On 13 November the prime minister wrote to his departmental head asking the taskforce to conduct a full examination of the advice provided by personnel involved in the incident, how the advice was obtained and conveyed, and the nature of advice provided to ministers and how it was transmitted. Moore-Wilton asked an assistant secretary in the department,

Canberra Times cartoonist Geoff Pryor's view of the relationship between public servants and senators

Jennifer Bryant, to undertake the review. A week later the chief of the defence force asked for a "routine inquiry" into the "proximate cause, events circumstances and imperatives" surrounding the SIEV4 rescue and all subsequent dealings. Here were at least two acknowledgements that all had not gone well. They might also be seen as attempts to preempt later parliamentary inquiries. For the next three months the officials collected evidence and wrote their reports. When they were tabled, the incident entered a new stage, as a parliamentary political football.

As soon as parliament reconvened after the election the Senate announced that it would establish a select committee to determine how truth went overboard. Because the government did not hold a majority in the Senate, it could not prevent a committee being established—as long as Labor and the Democrats agreed on the terms of reference and gained the support of an independent. Government senators, however, could participate fully and seek to turn the proceedings to their own benefit.

But Senate select committees have their problems, too. They can call some people but not others. All members of the House of Representatives and of state parliaments are protected. So, as a matter of convention, are ministerial staffers. Principally, committees can call public servants; but even then there are limitations. As the chair of the committee routinely reminds witnesses, public servants cannot be required to comment on government policy, although they may be asked to explain it. Consequently Senate committees examine one group of people, the public servants, in order to discover what another group, the ministers and their staff, actually did. The target of the opposition is always the ministers: they do not care much what the public servants did; they want to know what the ministers knew. But they cannot ask them. As a means of discovering what happened, it is far from ideal, but a Senate committee remains the best means of holding the government accountable that the system provides.

In this instance the opposition senators were looking for the "smoking gun" that would indicate that the prime minister, or at least some of his remaining ministers, knew the story of the children overboard was not true. Even if the initial story was based on advice, why was it not corrected? Inconveniently for the opposition, the defence minister, Peter Reith, had retired from parliament; his complicity would only be a secondary victory.

The government senators had a different agenda: to indicate that in every piece of potentially damaging evidence there is a reasonable doubt, or at least a different interpretation that makes it seem normal and innocent. They would try to run enough red herrings across the track to ensure that attention would be distracted. In this case they had extended the terms of reference to cover all the SIEV arrivals in that period, and they preferred to talk about all the other incidents in which the navy came into contact with refugees. If, they suggested, a pattern of hostile and violent behaviour existed, it mattered less if the one incident didn't occur; if similar outrages happened on other occasions, they implied, the characterisation of refugees as undesirable was warranted, and the investigation was a storm in a tea cup.

For the public servants and defence personnel appearing before the committee, the experience could be gruelling. Life at the top of the public service can be frenetic. Issues come on and off the agenda; ministers make demands; information circulates at speed. A conversation half listened to, a meeting interrupted by phone calls, briefings, queries; little time remains for notes or records which may be hastily jotted down as *aides memoire*. An official must provide advice and make decisions on a range of often disconnected issues. As ministers have become more imperious and often unreasonable, these actions take place in an environment that can be seen as precarious. The process may be neither neat nor predictable.

An inquiry is totally different. Here a subject is filleted. A single theme is extracted and followed through; this inquiry, after all, originated in a misinterpreted phone call, no more. Events have to be pulled out of the morass and given a logical sequence. A snatched conversation is deconstructed to discover every shade of meaning and intent. A meeting can be turned into a conspiracy. Words become weapons for analysis.

Public servants are obliged to provide accurate answers and not to mislead, but they are conscious that they still need to protect their political masters. Many of them will answer exactly what they are asked and no more—and then with precision and a careful choice of words. They will give away no more than they must. "The flatter the better" was the gist of the advice given to Jennifer Bryant in the prime minister's office when she was appearing before the Senate estimates committee. Her evidence provides a vivid example. She revealed that in the prime minister's office on that occasion, she talked to a few people who were around. Not until asked directly did she acknowledge that one of them was the prime minister! And all the time, faced with questions that could mildly be described as provocative, public servants must retain their cool; by convention senators must be treated with politeness. Only a retired admiral can use the forum to accuse senators of using weasel words.

Even before the select committee began its proceedings the opposition had used the estimates committees to investigate the players in this event. Those hearings extracted a number of pieces of information that had not appeared in the official reports. The head of the prime minister's department refused to accept that no children had been thrown overboard. He noted simply that the fact that there was, as yet, no evidence to support the case did not mean it had not occurred. The author of the Bryant report agreed she had not mentioned discussions she'd had with the prime minister's office; she had not recalled them. Most dramatically, Air Vice Marshall Houston informed the estimates committee that, in his capacity as acting chief of the defence force before the election, he had told the former minister that there was no evidence to support the story. On the same day of hearings the chief of the defence force said that he still believed the story was true. Three days later, after checking for the first time with the captain of the *Adelaide* and looking at the evidence, he held a press conference to admit that it had not happened. "Do you feel a dill?" he was asked by one journalist. It had taken the committee's questioning to make him look at the evidence.

The scene was set for the Senate Select Committee on a Certain Maritime Incident, which held hearings over four months from March to June. It began with the testimony of the secretary of the defence department, Allan Hawke. It questioned the captain of the *Adelaide* for two days, and grilled a parade of senior defence officers and public servants—with a highlight being the appearance of the chief of defence force warning that Australia was in danger of slipping into the third world war (and implying that the committee was a waste of his time). It summoned those officials from prime minister and cabinet involved in the taskforce. Some appearances were brief; others lasted for hours. Some were precise and confident in their recollections; others had memories so fallible, and could recall so little, that they generated biting cartoons in the press the next day.

For the opposition the chief investigator was Senate leader John Faulkner. He would begin slowly, with measured questions, circle the victim, rephrase the answers in terms he preferred, challenge interpretations, and then suddenly pounce. In front of him was a open laptop computer to which his staff, listening to proceedings elsewhere in Parliament House, could email suggested questions and comments on the evidence as it developed. Occasionally he was delighted with a discovery, such as Bryant's admission that she had talked to the prime minister during the estimates hearings. His approach was a combination of siege and sudden assault. The government's defence counsel was Queensland senator George Brandis, who described his approach as forensic. He showed all the skills of the barrister he had been in a former life; every event the opposition saw as sinister he portrayed as routine, every comment open to quite innocent interpretation. Bryant's meeting with the prime minister was no more than an accident. The reports from the *Adelaide* did not prove a child was *not* thrown overboard; most of them did not say anything about it at all, so they were not conclusive. Defending the government's actions by requiring that the other side to prove a negative gave him full scope for his skills.

The process was adversarial, the opposition on the attack, the government in defence. Both used standards of proof selectively to suit their case. The opposition took it for granted the prime minister knew, and they wanted a smoking gun. Even if they did not find that proof, that did not mean he did not know—a case of demanding the government prove another negative, that the prime minister did not know. The government senators argued that there was no proof, and that (in this case) this meant the prime minister did not know.

The hearings made the government and public servants

nervous. Cabinet decided that departments would not make submissions to the committee and that ministerial staff would not appear. In March the prime minister's office checked with Bryant that there was no way Scrafton's conversations with the prime minister would go any further. Defence established a taskforce to coordinate responses. Then Brendon Hammer and Harinder Sidhu from the prime minister's department invited the former liaison officer from Defence, Stefan King, to refresh their memories of what had happened. The first suggestion was that the meeting be held over the weekend at Hammer's home. Eventually they met in the coffee bar at the Hotel Kurrajong. Hammer offered to run a series of hypothetical questions and answers so that the defence officer, inexperienced in appearing before committees, could practise; the defence official thought they were really trying to discover what he would say, and declined to play. (No wonder the officials from the prime minister's department were concerned: the defence liaison officer thought he had formally briefed them; they had brushed it off as tea room gossip).This meeting became public when the defence department complained that it was an attempt to tamper with evidence. (The secretary of the prime minister's department, Max Moore-Wilton, ran an internal inquiry and found no evidence that anyone had behaved improperly.) The fear and politics, the publicity and gossip, was continuous.

And yet, within the limitations created by its incapacity to call ministers or their advisers, the select committee did uncover a range of accounts of what happened and how the story unfolded. Faced with selective memories, a lack of documentation, and the occasional missed opportunity it could never get the whole truth. But we know far more than we might have done without the process of investigation.

CHAPTER 3

Does our system work?

Ministers announced that children had been thrown overboard. They had been advised, by phone, that such an event had happened. They gave out the news in the most censorious and disapproving terms; it suited their agenda and made the headlines. The ministers released photographs to prove their case. But the story was wrong, and the public was never told so. The photographs were of another incident, but no retraction was ever made. Should the truth have been revealed and, if so, by whom?

We expect politicians to be "economical with the truth", in the real meaning of that term. That is, we expect them to spin a story of what they have done in such a way that it provides the best gloss and rebounds to their benefit. They may change the emphasis, leave out a few details, or make bold connections. What they say may be true but the announcement is designed to mislead, to provide a certain impression. No one would be surprised by such a strategy. But we do not expect them to lie, and if they have misled the public we might expect them to correct their story. Indeed, Howard's own ministerial code stipulates that misleading statements be corrected when the truth is discovered. It should not merely be a pious hope.

Here the public was told, on the front pages of the newspapers, that refugees had thrown children overboard. Within three days dozens of people within government knew the story to be false. Who should have changed the picture?

Not the military, it seems—even at the level of basic facts. In evidence before the Senate committee, military officers noted one after the other that giving information to the media was not their responsibility. That, they argued, should occur further up the chain of command. Commander Banks was reprimanded for talking to Channel 10 at all, even though he only answered a call on the navy's communication system and was careful not to respond to any question that might relate to future actions or policy. Australia was not at war with the refugees; it was a rescue operation. To a citizen it does not seem unreasonable that the country should be told how well its navy had performed. After all, it had been the ministers who had chosen to blast the rescue of refugees overboard across the front pages of the press, and they should not have been surprised that reporters wanted to speak to the commander on the spot.

Banks himself was warned by his military superiors to say nothing. "I was readily advised to keep very quiet", he told the select committee, adding that Admiral Smith had told him "he had been effectively gagged so that I should think nothing of staying quiet". He told the committee that, when he had "become adamant" that no children had been thrown overboard, he asked his superiors:

> [D]id I need to do anything about that? And the answer was, "no, that will be dealt with at other levels". I think I may even have spoken about did I need to send another signal or did I need to send a letter to the press. And the answer was no. By the time I got back to Perth on 14 October I had no uncertainty I was not to discuss it.

So much for supporting the commander on the spot. His statement of 10 October had been definite. It only reached the top when Houston asked for evidence in November. Why did it take so long?

Banks in turn warned his crew that they should not discuss these events outside official circles. No one raised the events with the prime minister when he visited the *Adelaide* before it was posted to the Gulf. They answered questions he put to them but did not elaborate. Given the warnings to stay quiet, it might have been galling but it is not surprising; sailors do not challenge prime ministerial truthfulness!

That attitude continued up the chain of command. Silverstone was concerned with what he should say to the minister as he was not aware of what "the system" might have told him. When he did comment that the video did not show any children being thrown overboard it was in response to a question from the minister. Indeed, he was surprised that the minister had not been told that there was no evidence to support that story. (In fact, of course, Reith had been told of the doubts, and appeared to be relying on the video remaining unseen to provide cover.) Without the initial question from the minister he did not regard it as his responsibility to raise the issue at all. "I work within a chain of command and I am required to perform within a chain of command."

His superior, Rear Admiral Smith, told the parliamentary secretary for defence about the story on 7 October because he happened to be in his company. He did not regard it as his responsibility to talk to the media: that was a matter for those further up the chain of command. Smith's superior, Rear Admiral Ritchie, took a similar view: "I am not in a position to say that people down the chain of command, such as I am, should have direct contact with government if I think that something that has been done is wrong." Instead, as he put it,

> I told the CDF [chief of the defence force] ... the CDF indicated that he would talk to the minister about it. I am not going to go and talk to anyone lesser in the chain. To me that is about as far as you can go ... Did I see fit to go forward and correct the record and my answer to that is no.

The chief of the navy, Admiral Shackleton, told the estimates committee and the select committee more than once that it was not his responsibility to tell the media the story was wrong and that there was no evidence to corroborate the initial accounts. He had told the chief of the defence force that the photographs had been misrepresented, but then left it to him to tell the minister and ensure the stories were corrected.

> My reason for not making any public comment on that was that it is for the CDF to change the advice to the government. It is not for the Chief of Navy to make public comments about those issues ... I provide advice, as do others, to the Chief of Defence Force and what matters is his opinion. I do not control what is going into the public space.

The chain of command thus led inexorably to Admiral Barrie, chief of the defence force. It was up to him to decide what would be said and how courageously the point would be pressed. As he described the situation to the estimates committee, "When it comes to Defence, with a capital D, I am it". That is where the buck stopped. He did advise the defence minister on 11 October that the photographs had been misinterpreted and that they referred to the sinking rather than to the overboard events of the day before. He said that the minister was "testy" at the news, a reaction that Barrie attributed to the minister being "angry because there had been a stuff-up over the photographs". A week later he did advise that there were "doubts" in Defence about the whole story, but stated he would not change his advice. That position allowed the minister to continue to insist he had been advised that children had been thrown overboard and—even after the call from Air Marshall Houston—to deny he had *formally* been advised otherwise by the chief of the defence force.

That was all Barrie did. He had required that statements be collected from the *Adelaide* crew, but did not ask for a report on the findings or see Banks's statement of 10 October. He "offered the opportunity" to his subordinates to correct the record, but that falls short of demanding to know the correct story so that he could advise the minister with precision. He would not comment on why the minister did not correct the public record. Nor does he record any other occasion on which he tried to correct the public account or persuade the minister to do so. He commented later: "The confusion about what the photographs represented was discussed with the minister. Why the public record was not changed I cannot answer." Indeed, it seems he did not want to know. Houston was able to absorb the data and advise the minister in a couple of hours. Barrie spent months. When Banks offered to talk about the incident in January, he was brushed aside. When Barrie appeared before the Senate estimates committee in February he still had not looked at the documents. So his comment that, as far as he was concerned, children had been thrown overboard, was welcomed by the prime minister as evidence that "Defence with a capital D" still thought it had happened. Not until he actually talked to Banks the following weekend and looked at the evidence was Barrie persuaded of the facts that everyone else had accepted months before. He then performed a humiliating public somersault. His stand had been convenient for the government; it allowed deniability to be sustained for weeks after it should have been told unequivocally what Defence knew.

At the very least, this record of insensitivity raised questions about Barrie's political nous. Given the choice between "no surprises" and a policy of letting sleeping dogs lie, he chose the latter. The costs might have been great. As a leader of the armed forces Barrie had a good record; the successes in East Timor and other commitments undertaken on his watch as chief of the defence force are a tribute to his leadership. About his capacity to be the chief adviser to government, this case raises questions.

All his subordinates put their faith in the chain of command to ensure that the government was adequately and forcefully advised on what had occurred. It did not work. Ritchie believed that the failure in Defence was not in the original account but in the failure to refute the information when it was found to be false. He wished "we had put it in writing on 11 October". Doubtless, after the event, so does everyone else. Nor was there ever an explanation of why Banks's statement of 10 October— categorical in its denial of the events—did not pass up the chain of command to the chief of the defence force. It was presented quickly in November when Houston asked for a briefing. Was this a failure in the chain of command?

Should Barrie have done more when it was clear that the minister was not going to correct the misinformation? Surely yes, for it was not only his minister who was being misled. The prime minister was on the record talking up the events, and public servants have obligations to the whole of government as well as to the individual minister. The essence of good advice is that there are no surprises, that ministers are warned about any potential problems. Indeed the requirement for "no surprises" was a creed mentioned by officers of the Department of Prime Minister and Cabinet. If it became clear that the story was untrue, even if there were just significant doubts about such a politically sensitive story, the prime minister's advisers should know. At the very least, Barrie should have checked the facts and then rung Max Moore-Wilton, secretary of the prime minister's department, to say that there might be problems with this issue, and that the prime minister needed to be aware of the doubts. What Moore-Wilton did with such information would then have been up to him.

What of the civilian side of Defence? The secretary of the department, Allan Hawke, argues that when the issues were about military operations they were the responsibility of Barrie. Hawke explained in a letter to the committee that, according to the directive from the minister on roles of the secretary of the department and the chief of the defence force, the latter was responsible for implementing the government's border protection policies and for reporting to the government. As secretary he was required to ensure his actions were not inconsistent with the chief of the defence force's role as principal military adviser. He wrote: "For my part, I believe it would have been quite wrong for me to have cut across the considered position of the CDF on the initial allegations by contradicting it before the Minister for Defence or, more especially, anyone outside Defence."

When the civilian side of Defence became involved, it was his responsibility. He ordered the head of Defence public affairs to tell the minister's office in writing about the photographs, but she did not. In retrospect, he believes that he ought to have done more and should have insisted on giving formal advice to the minister. He offered to resign, but his offer was not accepted. At least this was a recognition that someone should be responsible. The head of public affairs had ordered that all emails of the pictures be deleted to allow the minister to make the correction, but the correction never came. McKenry believed that a correction should have been made, but added: "I did not believe that it was my role or the role of anyone else to enter the public debate on the matter, the information having been provided to the minister's office and myself and Brigadier Bornholt being left in no doubt that the senior adviser understood quite clearly what those photographs represented."

In other departments there were no attempts to change anything. In effect, the subject was treated as concluded. But should it have been? According to the secretary of the immigration department, the people smuggling taskforce's job was "to bring together all the government agencies involved to respond to this phenomenon of illegal boat arrivals". It asked for information to corroborate the first account but it never checked what was available, even after questions were raised on the evening of the first day. There was no "caveat" to the statement, so the taskforce assumed it was correct. Nor was the taskforce given the chronology it requested, a document which also raised doubts about evidence. The attitude was to look for support, not to question. Yet it was a meeting of the taskforce that had considered "media lines" for the immigration minister when he rang on 7 October. After asking for the evidence, its members say they simply "moved on". Nothing, it seems, of the furore in Defence reached them. Yet this was the primary body collecting information.

The secretary of the prime minister's department was careful to explain to the estimates committee that his department had never been formally advised of the doubts. When he undertook to examine the charge of witness tampering against his staff, he saw fit to add in the report to the prime minister that was sent to the committee:

> I consider that it is worth restating that at no time did I seek to raise issues relating to "children overboard" with you prior to the November 2001 election. It remains my view that issues relating to "children overboard" were not central to this department's responsibilities in coordinating the Government's policy and operational responses in regard to illegal immigration by sea. At no stage did any officer within the Department of Defence or the ADF contact me to express concerns regarding "children overboard" prior to the election. For my part, I would not regard it as usual for Defence management to raise with me issues relating to the advice that they would provide to the Minister for Defence or his Office.

So, in his view, the prime minister's department was not formally told.

In the opinion of his predecessor, such a response was not adequate. Michael Keating, secretary from 1991 to 1996, told a seminar in June 2002 that one of the first duties of a public servant was to be sure that advice going to ministers was accurate. In this case, he considered there had been enough doubts about the accuracy of the information going to the prime minister that the most senior public servant should have sought assurance that the advice was correct. He should do that personally or through "a deputy secretary who understands your values".

For most departments there were other pressing matters to contend with after 11 October. Yet it was this issue that returned to plague the government. Senior public servants are expected to have good political (not partisan) antennae, but they were not working here. Too often, once information was passed on, correcting the story was not seen as their responsibility.

The British once had a way with unsuccessful admirals. They shot them on the quarterdeck for cowardice. Or rather they did it once, in 1757, when tardiness and excessive caution by Admiral John Byng led to the loss of Minorca. It was, declared Voltaire, *pour encourager les autres.* Governments are less dramatic today, but the lesson is still there. Public servants can lose their jobs if the government is not satisfied with their performance, or even if it simply does not like the way they work.

When the Howard government won office in 1996 it fired six departmental secretaries. Even if it believed that one or two of the casualties may have been politically connected, others clearly were not. They were career public servants who had been promoted from within the ranks and risen on talent, not as a result of political favours: this was the merit principle at work. But they went anyway.

There was nothing entirely new about the removal of secretaries; it had occurred on and off over the previous decade. Sometimes they were eased out, pushed into retirement or found alternative jobs. Sometimes a new face was wante; at other times, new initiatives and directions. Their title had been changed in 1984 from permanent secretary to departmental secretary; it was not just a cosmetic change. Permanence, a career in the one department, was gone; now, the secretaries could expect to be rotated every five years or so. Instead of each department growing its own managers, the public service was developing a band of generic managers who understood the need for a "whole of government" approach and could move from area to area with ease.

Then, in 1993, most of the secretaries were put on contract, with terms of up to five years, in exchange for a small rise in their salary. At the end of these contracts the government had no obligation to continue their employment; it could simply dispense with their services, thus forcing them to leave the public service.

Even so, the decision to terminate the contracts of six in one sweep, including those seen as career officials, not only surprised the public service community but also introduced a degree of apprehension. More cases followed. After the travel rorts affair led to the firing of three ministers, for instance, the Department of Administrative Services was abolished and the secretary's contract ended, even though it was the ministers who had abused the system.

But most startling was the sacking of the secretary of defence in 1999. Paul Barratt had been brought back into government in 1996 by the prime minister to head the Department of Primary Industries and Energy. He had been promoted to Defence when the secretary retired; it was a sign that he was performing well. But he did not get on with the new minister, John Moore, who took over after the 1998 election. Very quickly the minister sought to undermine him and then to have him fired. For a time he was protected by the secretary of the prime minister's department, but eventually selective leaks made his position, and that of the prime minister, impossible. In effect, the prime minister had to choose between supporting his minister and supporting the departmental secretary. He chose to back the minister for the time being, and terminated Barratt's contract.

Barratt took the government to court, arguing that he had done nothing wrong and nothing to warrant his sacking. The government argued that, in effect, secretaries of departments held their positions at the pleasure of the government; it did not have to give any reason to end their contracts. Indeed, in the appeal hearing both sides accepted that nothing Barratt had done had led to this situation. But the court found that if the minister had no confidence in the secretary, regardless of whether that lack of confidence was justified, the situation was not in the interest of good administration, and so the government could terminate his contract. The court case may have been intended to give some justice to secretaries, but instead it illustrated just how precarious their position could be. Admiral Chris Barrie was in the middle of that fight; one of the minister's complaints was that Barrie's wife was the secretary's executive assistant. Barrie had carried the messages, and sometimes the warnings; he knew well what the wrath of a minister might mean.

After 1999 the *Public Service Act* unequivocally stated that secretaries were appointed by the prime minister on such terms and conditions as he saw fit. They could also be terminated at will. That condition could well have introduced a degree of tension between secretaries and their ministers—particularly in Defence, where there was so recent an example of arbitrary execution.

Pour encourager les autres? There is an argument that firing a secretary every now and again has a salutary effect, making them all the more conscious of the need to be responsive to the needs and interests of the minister. They become acutely aware of the trapdoor that could suddenly open under them. In turn the pressures on secretaries influence the attitude and practices of those on the next one or two rungs of the public service; they reflect the values and often the style of their bosses. Consequently, the argument goes, senior officials are less likely to tell ministers what they need to know and are more inclined to pull their punches, even to fudge the bad news, fearful that the messenger might be shot. They no longer give the frank and fearless advice that was reputed to be the hallmark of the public service.

The legendary example of frank and fearless advice concerns the time when Sir Frederick Wheeler, secretary of the Treasury, gave prime minister Gough Whitlam details of the loans affair that would eventually help bring down his government. When Whitlam seemed disinclined to listen, Wheeler is reputed to have said, "You will listen to me because your government may depend on it", or words to that effect. It was a brave and necessary stand, and deserves its place in the myths and legends of the public service. But we should not assume from that incident that, in days gone by, all ministers were told everything they wanted or needed to know.

On the contrary, there were times when public servants chose not to tell ministers details they thought it better that they *not* know. Take the same public servant, Sir Frederick Wheeler. In 1974 the Treasury's principal budget submission was written in such a way as to conceal its more drastic potential effects. The purpose was to persuade more than inform. So frustrated did Malcolm Fraser become at his inability to extract the data he wanted when he was prime minister that he split the Treasury into two departments, Treasury and Finance, in 1976. The Treasury protected information because it knew, as did Fraser, that information was power.

In these instances public servants decided what they thought it best that ministers should know. They had a policy line they wanted adopted, and they used such vehicles as they could to win that case. All advice is selective. It requires a degree of discretion from public servants in determining what information the minister should receive.

What, then, is frank and fearless advice? It means telling ministers what they need to know, even when the news is bad and even when ministers may not want to hear it. But always within a context. It does not mean that the secretary insists on a policy agenda that is different from that of the government. It does not mean that the department obstructs when it cannot persuade the ministers to accept its proposals. There is nothing wrong in a department taking into account the policy directives of the government, or indeed the interests of the government. Policy advice which, while apparently correct, skewers the government is unlikely to be accepted. Advice will always be contingent on the circumstances and the directions of the government.

In giving advice the public service may decide on the best solution and, quite properly, present that solution as an option for the government. But the public service has no special position by which it can determine the national interest over and above the position taken by the government. The *Guidelines on Official Conduct* stipulate that advice be given "within government policy". They can advise, cajole, and persuade, but in the end the appointed officials can, and should, take second place to the elected ministers. Advisers need to know how far they can insist on having their say and where the dividing line is between pressing an argument and nagging. As the epigrammatic public service sage, Mick Shann, put it: "To object once is obligatory, twice is necessary, three times is suicidal." As long as the ministers have the intellectual and personal authority to make the decisions their view will usually prevail.

There should be one basic rule: as far as possible there should be no surprises for ministers. Public servants should anticipate anything that may go wrong. They should be able to warn the minister of dangers down the track, and to do that demands a degree of reflection and careful consideration. Most ministers would welcome such a service. They do not wish to be surprised; they want to be in control of events, to know what questions are being asked, what the implications might be, and who will win or lose from the introduction of a new policy. To provide that service is not to be partisan; it is to serve the government.

So far the discussion has been about providing advice, because that is the area where expertise and values may intrude, and where careful calculations are required. In this case it was, perhaps, even simpler. The issue was not whether something was desirable, but what had happened. The facts may have been in dispute initially, but within Defence, at all those levels below chief of the defence force that had chosen to check them, there was no support for the story. There can be no case for not telling the ministers the facts or, if they are in dispute, getting them right. Here they were assumed, then challenged, but never adequately checked.

If accidents happen, if things go wrong, ministers need to know before they hear about it in the media. Responses must be prepared, a strategy to explain and to fix must be mapped out. And most of the time something will go wrong. The sour law of unintended consequences (gloriously called *slucs*) strikes every policy. Society does not run on the laws of physics; people are unpredictable, bloody-minded, and capricious. What policy makers predict often fails to happen. How, then, can the advisers cope? They must make sure of the evidence on which advice is based and then ensure it is correct again.

Not this time. *Slucs* did indeed occur. They began with a series of miscommunications; what the commander thought was "threatening to throw a child overboard" became "throwing a child overboard", which metamorphosed into "children overboard" and hence a high-profile story that would be embarrassing to correct. Whether the problems were caused by "the fog of war" or just a muddle, a false story became a fact that then had to be disproved, not merely checked. That is the worrying factor of this case: the mindset.

Does this make senior public servants political? Is the public service politicised? Although it is sometimes claimed that senior officials have been appointed because they have party affiliations, there is little evidence to support that view. In 2001 the new head of the industry department was appointed from the Confederation of Australian Industry, but that type of appointment is rare. Occasionally secretaries have become, deliberately or not, so identified with the government that it would be difficult to imagine that they would readily be able to serve a government of a different party; but that, too, is rare.

Most senior bureaucrats fit neither of these two categories. Traditionally they have regarded themselves as career officials who will serve each government with equal dedication. They are not neutral between government and opposition—their role is to serve the government—but they are equally dedicated when a government has changed. Their role is to be responsive to the government. They would regard themselves as determinedly non-political.

Has that position changed? In one respect, no; most of the heads of departments are still selected from within the public service. They have worked through the ranks of the service, and are regarded as the best available. But they can no longer be certain that they will remain in their position. Over the past twenty years their position has become more uncertain; the trapdoor is an ever-present threat if the minister has become unhappy with their performance. For some, that threat makes no difference; they say what they think and are prepared to live with the results. For others, it means that bad news must be couched in more careful terms—that they will roll with the punches and come back again to tell the ministers what they need to hear. Eventually the message gets through. Some may decide that if the ministers do not want to hear bad news or contrary advice they will not give it. Of course, everyone puts themselves into the first two categories: fearless or strategic. No one will admit to being cowed. In truth, it will be a matter of character.

The contracts themselves may have an impact because senior officials know now that if the minister has "no confidence" in them, they are gone. But the contracts do more than that. Initially all the contracts were for five years, providing a degree of stability as well as equal treatment for all. Now they are more selective. The prime minister can give contracts for "a period of up to five years", and it appears that those with the closest ties to the government, those in greatest favour, get five years; others get three years. It is divisive and shows a lack of confidence. Keeping the government's main advisers in a state of uncertainty is hardly a recipe for good advice.

One demand is rather more insidious. It is the belief on the part of governments—all governments—that they want not only support but *passion* from their public servants. When a leading American political scientist was comparing Washington and Whitehall in the 1960s he was asked by a bright young Treasury official from Britain, "Why are your officials so passionate?" (And he was referring to staff in the budget bureau in Washington, perhaps the least passionate people there.) Why? Because senior American officials are not careerists: they are there for a time, and perhaps a cause. British, and Australian, public servants have traditionally been the more useful because they are required to be dispassionate. They could not serve all masters if they cared desperately who was governing. When an Australian minister complained that the public servants did not seem to approach their role with passion, he was told that their job required dispassionate analysis and advice: responsive, aware of the political environment, balanced, and wise. Problems would come if passionate public servants disagreed with the programs of governments.

Yet often governments still feel that they cannot be served

well unless the public servants *believe* in their policies. They view the senior officials who served the previous regime with suspicion because, believers themselves, they find it hard to comprehend that a public service can serve without passion. And, as public service careers begin to rely more and more on the good favours of ministers, departmental secretaries can become too responsive, too concerned to show they are on board, too concerned with political protection. Prophesies can become self fulfilling. And the fabric of the public service can be harmed.

In his Garran Oration in 1998 the prime minister stated:

> No government "owns" the public service. It must remain a national asset that services the national interest, adding value to the directions set by the government of the day. The responsibility of any government must be to pass on to its successors a public service which is better able to meet the challenges of its time than the one it inherited. My government clearly accepts that responsibility.

Perhaps he should remind his ministers—and, perhaps even more so, their advisers—of that statement.

Of course, during this affair the public servants all assured the committees they had behaved properly. Let two speak for the many. Jane Halton stated:

> Let me address the issue [of politicisation] directly. I am absolutely confident that this committee [the people smuggling taskforce] behaved extremely properly in terms of information management and issue management. It was explicitly and deliberately careful. I have already made a reference to the fact that issues in relation to the caretaker conventions were as appropriate canvassed on the

odd occasion. I cannot go into specifics, but I do recall that. As a public servant of 20 years standing, I am very familiar with the APS [Australian public service] code of conduct and values. I am absolutely confident that the discussion in those meetings and the behaviour I observed and certainly of my officials was very proper.

Admiral Barrie, too, was keen to protect himself from the charge he had been politicised:

> To the contrary I regard my role as apolitical but, subject to my obligation under the Defence Act, faithfully and with complete integrity to serve the government of the day, whatever its political persuasion. As I have said before this is essential to the functioning of our democracy. Because the allegation has been made I want to emphasise the priority I place on the need for impartiality ... I did not receive direction from any minister, or anyone else for that matter, to ignore or not follow up the issue of whether children had been thrown overboard from SIEV4.

To adapt Mandy Rice-Davies's immortal words: "They would say that, wouldn't they?" But the point is not whether they attend a Liberal Party fund raiser or a Labor Party conference. Rumours that senior officials would enter a taskforce meeting declaring "now we've won the election" make good stories but are surely apocryphal. The question is whether they were so concerned to serve the government of the day— which seemed likely to be the government for the foreseeable future— that the urge to serve overpowered the need to be critical. Halton and some of her colleagues reveal a mindset so determined to find evidence to corroborate the story that they glossed over the evidence pointing the other way. It was an attitude of mind, not a conspiracy. Then the issue went off the radar. It should not have needed warning bells and red lights, particularly in the defence force where the questions were asked, to know it might resurface and the truth might out.

The charge, then, is not that the public service has been politicised in a partisan sense, but that public servants were politically inept in an advisory sense—that they were too keen to serve, and not sufficiently sceptical and alert to warn.

Ministerial staff have grown in influence and importance over the past twenty years, to the extent that they have long outgrown existing procedures for accountability and responsibility. They are now the black hole of government, unaccountable in practice, even if not in theory.

Originally appointed to assist ministers with the running of their offices, ministerial staff had a very limited advisory role and no authority. But gradually, initially during the Whitlam government and increasingly since, that changed. Ministers wanted more help. They did not trust the bureaucracy, and wanted around them people who were on their side, who saw things from their viewpoint. They wanted partisans, committed to their success and that of the government, party operatives whose future depended on the continuation of the government. So the number of staff grew and their influence expanded.

Often ministers' staff were on secondment from the departments the ministers headed. Departmental liaison officers were appointed to keep the lines of communication open. Senior advisers—on international relations or on military affairs, for example—provided expertise within the minister's office. The intention was that such people would not become involved in partisan politics; they would provide insight and information rather than a political perspective. But such neat lines were often difficult to draw; besides, as the officials became drawn into the daily activity of the office, there was always the danger that they would "go native" and begin to identify more with the minister.

Whether partisan or official, these officers are covered by the constitutional myth that they are no more than an extension of their ministers. They are appointed by the minister, they have no security of tenure, and they are in a job only as long as the ministers are in office.

Two assumptions initially grew from their standing. First, because they acted in the ministers' name, officials assumed that when they asked for information or advice, it was, in effect, the minister who was asking. Second, informing an adviser was regarded as the same as informing the minister. If the adviser knew, the minister knew. The consequence of these two assumptions was that advisers were protected from parliamentary inquiry; they could not be called before committees or forced to answer questions. As they were no more than an extension of the ministers, the ministers were accountable for all their actions.

That was fine as theory but has long been overtaken by a different reality. Forty or more people, including a spread of advisers, now speak—or are spoken to—in the prime minister's name. Obviously they collect a range of information that is not passed on to him; their role is to act as a sieve, deciding what the prime minister needs to know, asking departments for supporting data to bolster the briefs they provide. There is nothing wrong with that; prime ministers need help. But the advisers are also likely to be highly protective of the prime minister; there are things, they will believe, that he is better off not knowing—particularly if the new data contradicts a stand already taken in public.

The same is true for ministers. Their offices are smaller, but they are just as partisan. The staff are not simply a conduit for information to and from the ministers; they often seek it out. Increasingly, too, the staff have become more aggressive, more peremptory, more demanding. They do not merely contact the head of a department, but will range widely throughout the department, demanding information and wanting it immediately. Ministers cannot know what they ask; often the advisers seek to anticipate what ministers may want. They are an additional source of advice on policy, and will force their departmental advisers to justify their proposals and make them earn their place at the advisory table. When they have a sense of urgency they brook nothing but instant action. They have been known to scream down the phone. Often they are young, perhaps inexperienced in the ways of government. But they would no longer agree they have no executive authority. In the minister's name they demand action. And the way they do it may well reflect the style of their master. The behaviour of the minders is a mark of the minister.

In an evocative American phrase, some advisers have become the "junk-yard attack dogs" of the political system: the hard men and the hit men. They are politically dispensable, convenient scapegoats who will take the bullet for their ministers and protect them from political fallout. At different times, staffers from the prime minister's office and the deputy prime minister's office have resigned as a means of preventing scandal from touching their masters. In each case they had information that, they said, they'd failed to pass on to the minister. A lack of action was sheeted home to them, not to the ministers, and so they resigned (and were usually found comfortable billets thereafter). In defensive and aggressive postures, ministerial staff have been a boon to ministers on both sides of politics.

We can no longer maintain the myths that advisers are no more than an extension of ministers, and that telling the advisers is the same as telling the minister. We can no longer pretend that ministers know all that their advisers know. Nor, as a consequence, should we continue to protect ministerial staff from accountability by assuming that they are just an extension of the minister, and that they are therefore accountable through their ministers. History has long overtaken convention and practice.

The children overboard case illustrates just how far the practices have changed over the past twenty years. In all the accounts, the flow of information leads to the minister's office and then seems to dry up. At that point it becomes much harder to discover who was told what. And if they were told, did they pass it on or did they decide that it was preferable that the minister should not know so that it could be plausibly denied?

The principal example in this case was the media adviser to the Minister for Defence, Ross Hampton. He started in a special position. The minister had instructed that no one in Defence was authorised to make any public comments about Operation Relex. All media inquiries were to be directed to Hampton. Here was the modern phenomenon of political spin. Every news statement had to have the imprint of the government's message. Hampton wanted to ensure that any coverage of the refugees was couched in terms favourable to the case being put by the government. He not only told the defence department not to release photographs that would identify the refugees, according to a senior officer he instructed them to withhold photographs that "humanised or personalised" asylum seekers.

But Hampton was also driven by the daily news cycle. The media wanted comment, pictures, and the most recent reports. His job was to get them and then "spin them". But his timelines were always shorter and more pressing than those of the Defence officials. Clashes between the different imperatives was almost inevitable. They duly happened—often. As soon as he knew there were photographs of the SIEV4 incident, Hampton demanded copies. Insistent on immediate service and plagued by his computer's inability to open some emails, he eventually received two photos from media liaison in Defence. They had titles, but lacked the captions that identified when and where they were taken. But by 10 October he had been told via a message on his answering machine that the photos were of the sinking on 8 October. He never returned the call, and says he never received it. But he did, later, demand further copies. The strategic communications adviser to the chief of navy noted:

> Approximately one week after the release of the photos to the media via interaction between DML [Defence media liaison] and the Minister's Office, I received an agitated call from Minister Reith's Press Secretary, Ross Hampton. He told me that DML could no longer find the photographs and wanted me to send them to him. I found this disturbing. I advised him that I would check with HPACC [the head of the Defence public affairs division] first despite knowing they were already in the public domain. **He advised me in an aggressive tone that he was HPACC's boss and my boss as well and that I'd "better send them to him immediately".** He gave me no reason as to why he wanted them again and would not let me hang up until he had received them by e-mail. I sent the photos with captions under extreme duress and informed HPACC immediately. **My only solace was that by then the photos had been in the public domain for up to a week.** [Bold type in the original]

Of course Hampton was not the " boss" of any public

servant, but the peremptory tone of the demand put officials under great pressure. The Powell inquiry commented that "the multiple communication entry points used by the Media Adviser to contact any area or individual within the ADO … contributed to the degradation" of the intelligence provided to ministers.

At a later point another adviser, Reith's chief of staff, Peter Hendy, rang the chief of navy, Vice Admiral Shackleton, when he had been quoted as having disagreed with the minister and demanded that the point be clarified. It was, tightly and carefully.

Mike Scrafton, senior adviser (defence) in Reith's office, was on secondment from the defence department. He, too, played a significant role. In a statement to the Bryant inquiry Scrafton stated that "he had been involved in or aware of a number of discussions between Mr Reith's office and the Prime Minister's Office and the Prime Minister which he could not discuss". As a statement it was tantalising if uninformative. Since the prime minister's office had checked with Bryant in March to ensure this statement could not be taken further and the contents of these conversations would not be revealed, it must have been concerned about possible revelations. Scrafton had been told by Defence public affairs on 10 October that the photographs were of the wrong event, and by Ritchie that there were doubts about whether any children had gone overboard at all.

Scrafton understood the value of ensuring that a level of ambiguity was retained. When the secretary of the department, Dr Allan Hawke, realised that the published photographs were of the wrong occasion, he instructed that the minister be informed in writing of the problem. The head of Defence public affairs spoke to Scrafton and, instead of providing a formal minute, merely emailed further copies of the photos. In effect, she obeyed the adviser in preference to her departmental secretary. Hawke was informed but did not follow it up. It was still possible for the minister's office to say that it had not been advised formally of the error. Advisers could act in protective mode; they could determine what advice they wanted and, more significantly perhaps, what advice they did not want.

Scrafton was again involved when the issue blew up in the first week of November. He was asked by the minister to view the video film of the overboard incident. He watched the film and "considered that the tape clearly didn't show that the incident had happened". But, he added, "neither did it provide conclusive evidence that the incident didn't happen".

> Mr Scrafton stated that the Prime Minister rang him later that evening. He said he spoke to the Prime Minister a couple of times that evening about the tape and informed him that it was inconclusive.

This briefing was part of the process by which the prime minister prepared for the traditional Press Club appearance in the last week of the election campaign.

In general, there seemed to be a lack of trust between the department and the minister's office. Chief of staff Hendy noted:

> A lot of commentary in Defence had to be verified because Defence was an organisation that lived on gossip and rumour. There was a systemic problem with checking of facts, and the organisation lacked discipline in dealing with facts, confidentiality and public commentary. In this case faced with a range of stories (particularly in relation to the photographs) the minister's staff had to take everything they heard with a pinch of salt.

DOES OUR SYSTEM WORK?

Canberra Times cartoonist Geoff Pryor's response to the offer by the secretary of defence, Allan Hawke, to resign over the children overboard affair (above) and his comment on the issue of "deniability"

Hampton argued that criticisms of his mode of operation were not sustainable. He said it was:

> [s]tandard practice for me to contact, on behalf of the minister, senior officials with carriage of particular programs or operations to ensure the best possible advice possible—indeed the Minister often contacted the same individuals I did ... [F]inally it should be said that if the statement implies the Ministers (through their Media Advisers) should not seek information from senior Departmental officials, but always utilise public affairs officers, it is an unsustainable finding.

Such a stand may have some validity, but it is the inconsistent activity that may well tell a story. We have seen the vigour (to put it politely) with which advisers demanded information from officials. When asked if the minister had considered retracting the story presented by the photographs, Hampton told the Bryant inquiry "that it was between the Minister, Mr Hendy and Mr Scrafton and that he couldn't comment on what consideration if any was given to a retraction". (Note that in his turn Scrafton thought it was the minister and Hampton making that decision!). In Bryant's words, Hampton said that he believed:

> that the Minister requested advice clarification from Defence, although Ms Bryant would have to check this with Mr Hendy or Mr Scrafton ... Mr Hampton did not know whether the advice had been received. As far as Mr Hampton was aware there was no formal advice provided.

Again the emphasis on formal advice! It was an interesting phrase and, of course, selective. Advice over the phone was regarded as adequate to tell the story in the first place. And had the minister's office wanted that formal advice in a hurry they would have been very insistent in demanding that it be provided the same day. When Hampton wrote a note later to the Powell inquiry in November, he did not know if formal advice was ever provided; nor did he seem to care much. That was not typical of his earlier behaviour.

The secretary of the defence department, Allan Hawke, told the select committee that he felt he "could have done more on that issue by talking directly to the minister and by providing him with clear, written advice". "Relying on staffers in this case," he conceded, "was simply not good enough, so I have learnt a very hard lesson from that".

Asked by the chair of the committee whether he regarded contacting a ministerial adviser as equivalent to contacting the minister, he responded as follows:

> HAWKE: Each minister tends to have different rules of engagement. Some ministers would regard it as such; Senator Hill does not.
> CHAIR: What was the situation applying at the time? If you spoke to the media adviser, was it regarded that you were passing information to the minister?
> HAWKE: Yes, we would have been working on the assumption that that adviser would have had any necessary discussion with the minister. That may be a wrong-founded assumption.

The prime minister's own staff had also been active. Miles Jordana was a career public servant on secondment to the prime minister's office as adviser on international affairs. When the story initially broke, he sought additional details, but was apparently satisfied when the photos were published. He became involved again after the *Australian* argued that the incident may never have occurred. On the evening of 7 November he rang Bryant to request information for the prime minister's press club appearance. In particular, he wanted the relevant situation reports from the *Adelaide* and other information about the operation. He also contacted ONA—the Office of National Assessments—to find out what their sources were for its 9 October briefing. ONA responded in writing that the briefing was probably based on the comments of ministers, but they would check back to discover if there were any Defence sources. (On 12 November ONA told the prime minister's office there were not any Defence sources.) Jordana also had two phone conversations with deputy secretary of the prime minister's department, Jane Halton, about the "tea room gossip" in Defence that the photographs were wrongly identified; he assured her that the prime minister's office was on the job.

Which parts of this information were passed on to the prime minister? We do not know. Perhaps there are nudges and winks from the ministers which hint that they do not need to be told about these things. Perhaps "the rule of anticipated reactions" may come into play, with advisers deciding what ministers might, or might not, want to know, particularly at a time when an election is being held. After all, better to be told after the election is won that the information should have been passed on than pass it on and potentially embarrass the minister. Ministers can always say after the event that they were merely saying what they had been advised and that they were never told the contrary. And they did.

Neither of the internal inquiries came close to uncovering what the advisers said or did. Their main purposes were to examine the official activities below ministers' offices. The Defence exercise was a routine inquiry, and made a number of findings to be taken into account on future occasions. Bryant said that ministers were outside her purview. So, too, as a logical consequence, were their staff. She took information from them only as a means of better understanding where the official actions may have gone wrong.

The Senate inquiry got no closer to ministers or their staff. Three times it requested that the former minister of defence appear. Each time he refused. While it is certainly true that the Senate cannot call members of the House of Representatives before its committees, whether former ministers are immune is disputed. The committee also asked Jordana, Hendy, Scrafton, and Hampton to appear and received, in response, a refusal from the prime minister's chief of staff. "I advise," he wrote, "that in accordance with the decision of cabinet, which itself reflects longstanding practice under governments of both political persuasions, *Members of Parliament Staff Act* personnel and public servants who were in that category will not appear."

That may be a convention, but it could be disputed. In advice to the committee, the clerk of the Senate argued that:

> There is no law which prevents a legislative committee summoning ministerial advisers and personal staff. There is no parliamentary rule which prevents such a course. There is no convention that the legislature should always refrain from summoning such people.

The clerk of the House of Representatives disagreed, proposing that the immunity of ministers also applied to their staff. A legal opinion was sought from Brett Walker SC, and he advised that ministerial advisers "have no constitutional, statutory or principled claim to be less susceptible to the demands of the Senate than any other person". Nor, he argued, were former ministers exempt.

Neither the government senators nor their opposition counterparts on the select committee wanted to test the resolve of the government or the advice of officials. The Democrat committee member was on his own in wishing to use the powers of the Senate.

That is unfortunate. There is a strong argument that ministerial advisers *ought* to have been called before the committee. As the evidence makes clear, the argument that they are no more than the extension of the ministers' persona cannot be sustained. Ministerial advisers acted independently to organise media strategies, to determine the shape and tone of media releases, and to make judgements about what information should be pushed forward.

The core of the argument against calling them is that the operations of a ministerial office would become impossible if everything that was said was liable to exposure before a Senate committee partly made up of political opponents. But exactly the same case can be made for protecting senior officials. They need to be able to give the ministers frank and fearless advice. They need to express their views and to argue the case. Both are paid for by the public. Both have a recognised role. Yet one can be called and cross-examined while the others, who may well hold the secrets, are not. If a set of guidelines to cover the appearance of public servants can be devised that includes rules on what they can or cannot be asked, it should be possible to develop similar guidelines for ministerial staff. It could exclude questions about political advice, but could—indeed *should*—include information about relations with departments and accounts of what happened to the advice provided to the minister. Only that way can the notion that telling the advisers equals telling the ministers be tested.

Why hasn't this happened? Largely because it is not in the

interests of both the major political parties. Opposition members always hope that one day they will be back in government, and they do not want the discussions in their offices open to investigation any more than a current government. Consequently the myth that the staff are no more than an extension of the minister, however unrealistic, serves a useful purpose. And staff are always dispensable.

This situation was exacerbated by the rules that had been laid down for access to the media. In a circular of 8 August 2001 the secretary and the chief of the defence force promulgated a set of rules for speaking to the media that greatly limited access. For Operation Relex, these were made more restrictive; defence personnel, regardless of rank or position, were forbidden from making contact with the media. Defence public affairs was to coordinate all releases. But it, too, was constrained. All communications had to be cleared by the minister's office, which in these circumstances meant the media adviser, Ross Hampton.

The strategy had been drafted by Defence public affairs and discussed with the staff of the minister's office—first with Hampton and then with Hendy and Scrafton. There was only one set of proposals the minister's staff were prepared to accept, and that was one which effectively gagged all members of Defence up to and including the chief of the defence force. Every inquiry from the media was to be directed to Hampton. When a public affairs officer was sent to Christmas Island to help deal with the media there, Hampton demanded he be recalled. In Defence public affairs there was a dedicated phone from the ministers' office, and Hampton would ring ten to fifteen times a day and get absolute priority.

The minister's office also wanted to control all the pictures that were released from the Relex operation. While Immigration argued that photos should not identify individual refugees, Hampton went further, telling the Defence public affairs that he did not want any "humanising or personalising" pictures released. Reith's chief of staff, Peter Hendy, admitted that "he was aware some defence personnel perceived themselves as having been gagged, but said they often lacked an awareness of the fact that they might not be in possession of the whole story"— or the story as the minister's office wanted it portrayed.

Defence objected to the minister's restrictions but could do little about them. When the rules were relaxed in February 2002, Rear Admiral Ritchie "applauded" the new guidelines before the Senate committee, making it clear what he thought of the old ones. It was indeed odd that a Defence spokesperson could inform the media what was happening to Australian troops in Afghanistan but not say anything about what was happening on Australia's northern border. Admittedly Defence might always have regarded itself as a special case in its relations with the media. The head of Defence public affairs told the Powell inquiry that there was:

> a cultural belief that it is almost a right for defence personnel to interact and tell their story to the media. There is a culture that does not treat P[ublic] A[ffairs] guidelines and directives seriously and there are no visible sanctions for those who disregard public speaking directives.

Regardless, here was a remarkable attempt to limit all information to that which had the prescribed political spin. The criterion for release would not be national security alone, although that doubtless continued to apply. It was to be political advantage.

If there was ever a document that illustrated the degree to

which the government sought to use all the events to its political advantage it was this directive that all the data be sent through, or cleared with, the minister's office. When combined with the instinctive reliance on the chain of command and the decision of the chief of the defence force to say it once and then leave it to the minister to decide whether the public would continue to be misled, the outcome can only be regarded as unhealthy. If the country were at war, the public would expect this degree of control. But it was not; nor were the refugees behaving like terrorists. There is a distinction between the activities of the military in peacetime and those of wartime. News management, the political spinning of all stories to the exclusion of accuracy or completeness, is not new, but it has become an international concern as it has become all-pervasive and blatant. This case shows why that concern is warranted. Should a government be able to argue that it, and it alone, can determine what we know of its activities? Should all releases be carefully screened for political benefit? It is a dangerous precedent, especially during an election campaign.

Special rules—the caretaker conventions—apply to the relations between the government and the public service during an election campaign. By convention, the government will initiate no new policies and make no appointments. That part is easy to see and police. Ministers are also obliged not to use public servants in a partisan way. As a recent study put it: "Ministers remain nominally in charge of departments during an election campaign. They are still entitled to seek information on matters of fact, but cannot use the resources of the public service to partisan advantage."

In this instance there was an interesting gap in timing. The prime minister announced the election at the end of the week, but stated that the caretaker conventions would apply from the issue of the writs on the next Tuesday. It was in that gap, over the weekend, that SIEV4 arrived and ministers were informed that children were thrown overboard. There was an election on, but the convention nominally did not apply.

Would it have mattered? Probably not, for the public servants drew the distinction between the continuing implementation of an existing program and the initiation of the new one. As Halton put it:

> We need to be clear that there was a stated government policy that the people in this taskforce were working on the implementation of in terms of the information exchanged in that group and individually within agencies. They had been given clear riding instructions about the policy. The policy was set before the election was called … I think the taskforce at all times operated in an operational way. It did not operate in any sense in a way which went to a change in policy or to behaving improperly.

During an election campaign the easy interaction between ministers and public servants no longer occurs. The head of the Department of Immigration, for example, revealed that, after he advised his minister of the incident by phone, "the next contact I recall with the minister's office was not until 7 November" when the *Australian* article created a furore.

Moore-Wilton explained more fully:

> The caretaker convention provides that the Public Service is particularly conservative and sensitive to the advice it provides during an election campaign. The contacts between ministers and prime ministerial offices and the Public Service during that time is heavily constrained—appropriately so—so the advice and

issues cannot be used in a political context. All my officers in the Department of the Prime Minister and Cabinet are very aware of that. So the department is very careful about giving blow-by-blow information on the issues which may or may not be politically sensitive at the time, and to confine itself to the facts or new issues emerging which relate to the administration of government.

The problem is that the public servants have little control over how that information is used. Defence secretary Hawke stated that during the caretaker period "our role was to provide factual advice about what happened. What they do with that is up to the minister and the minister's office." In election mode the party officials take over much of the prime ministerial attention, and public servants have much less access. Readier access may have changed the situation and made it easier to insist on accurate data. The "I was advised" excuse would be harder to sustain if there was regular interaction between ministers and departments, as such a line would probably send out warning bells. Not here.

As it is, the limitations created by the caretaker conventions are still comparatively few. Even when it is done even-handedly, implementing government policy can help the governing party during an election campaign. But government cannot suddenly cease. The taskforce vigorously denied timing some of its decisions so that they did not clash with the launch of the Liberal campaign. It did not have to; merely doing its job was beneficial for the Liberal campaign. In elections, incumbency is a great advantage.

The original story was passed by phone from ship to taskforce to ministers. The only written advice was the sentence in the report sent to the prime minister and others on the evening of

7 October. Yet bureaucracy is renowned for being smothered in red tape, overwhelmed by paper. Not this time, clearly. Indeed, so little was committed to paper that it should be a cause for concern.

The taskforce was established after a corridor conversation between Moore-Wilton and Farmer. There were no terms of reference, and a fluid agenda and membership. Asked if the lack of a "paper trail" was worrying, Farmer responded:

> For me, no. I am concerned with effectiveness and with outcomes. That means I am concerned about paper trails where there is a quite appropriate requirement for a paper trail in an audit or other sense, but successive governments have made it clear that they want a public service that is able to be flexible and get the job done. That, for me, does not mean producing huge mounds of paper; it means looking at what is the most appropriate and effective way of getting something done.

There speaks the modern public servant. In Defence, Air Vice Marshall Titheridge made a similar comment:

> It is difficult, if not impossible, during a period of several crises (unauthorised arrivals was just one at the time) to formally record all information that was passed by word of mouth (including telephone).

Public servants argue they must be able to trust their sources if the system is to work. Moore-Wilton argued:

> Public service officers have to rely on the advice they are given. Generally speaking, if there is an opportunity to double-check that advice they will. However, in a rapidly evolving situation, if

advice is given from a reputable source with appropriate authority they take that advice. They have no choice.

Not for the modern official the leisurely opportunity to write a note for file recording a conversation with colleagues or ministers and acting as a record if something later became controversial.

All that was available were the phone notes of participants, often shorthand scribbles intended as an *aide memoire* for the person taking the call rather than as material for the public record. The Senate committees asked whether a department's emails were kept and whether records of phone calls were maintained. Both were, for a period at least. But although phone call records will tell us who was called, they will never give a detailed account of what was said. And, of course, they will only record one person's involvement in a sequence of events. Adding to the paucity of written information is a concern about which documents are public and therefore "discoverable" under freedom of information legislation.

Combined with email, yellow stickers, and message banks, the changing culture is producing a new style of record keeping. But what is remarkable in this case is the amount of modern technology that went wrong. Voicemail messages were not received, or not remembered. Emails could not be opened. Radio phone calls interrupted operations. The conventions of government advising have not always kept up with modern communications technology, and that created a situation ripe for exploitation or muddle. Both happened in this case. Historians in the future will have loads of material, but—if this case is a typical example—little that tells us how the significant decisions were made.

CHAPTER 4
Accountability and Australian government

This book has looked at the actions of three groups of people: the public servants, the ministerial advisers, and the ministers. Hindsight makes judgements easy, it is true. We did not have to anticipate that this issue was going to be so sensitive, or to determine whether an issue was "off the radar" or not. But then, if these people are appointed on merit, they should have the capacity to do these things better than the rest of us.

Public Servants: Public servants and military officers took a piece of advice, in good faith certainly, and informed the ministers without checking its veracity. They knew it would be highly sensitive and politically charged; the election had been called two days earlier. Then those outside Defence looked for evidence to corroborate the claims. The mindset was that the charges were true; the officials just wanted evidence. From that point on, *any* evidence seemed to settle the issue. There was muted scepticism within the prime minister's department but it was ignored. Then the world, they said, moved on.

Too much seems to have been discarded in a rush. A briefing from Defence was dismissed as "tea room gossip". Referring to Halton's decision to leave a message on Moore-Wilton's answering machine telling him about the doubts in November, the prime minister commented, quite fairly: "If you really wanted to convey something that was critically important and was something that caused shock, I would have thought some attempt other than to leave a message on a voice mail was required."

As the secretary of the prime minister's department told the estimates committee, "one of the differences between a professional public service, Uncle Tom Cobleigh, the media and everybody else is that generally unless there is evidence we do not draw a conclusion". In this case the evidence was scant. They had nothing but the outcome of a line of phone calls on which to advise ministers, but that was seen as enough. But if the story was to be corrected, then hints, caveats, and messages on answering machines were never going to be enough to provide the certainty it apparently needed, even if these doubts had emerged within three days. Phone calls may never again be seen as adequate evidence, but they should not have been in this case either, without being carefully checked.

Defence did its best to correct the record internally. It discovered what had actually happened but then, at the top level, it wobbled. Barrie may not, indeed, have been convinced that children were not thrown overboard right through until February 2002. He may have been distracted by organising the "war against terrorism", even the oncoming third world war he was worried about. But his advice to the minister—that there were doubts that the children were thrown overboard, but he was not going to change his initial advice (or check further what had really happened)—was an example of having it both ways. The minister was told and the minister was not formally advised. The public servant had done the job and warned the minister, but not in such a way that the minister had to consider himself warned. The minister could continue to say he received no formal advice and continue to describe the events as absolute fact.

Nor did Barrie warn anyone outside Defence of the concern even though it had the capacity to engulf the prime minister. Talking to the prime minister's department was not talking to the media and was not forbidden under the Operation Relex guidelines. It is precisely an appreciation of what is likely to cause a problem that is the sign of good judgement in senior public servants.

At the Senate hearings almost everyone stated that they had acted professionally and in a non-partisan way. Moore-Wilton unequivocally told the estimates committee that he had "seen no fact—I have seen a lot of assertions—which would warrant me to discipline any officer in my department". An internal inquiry in Department of Prime Minister and Cabinet about attempts to discuss evidence with a Defence witness found no evidence of improper behaviour. One or two of those involved thought they should have put their concerns in writing, but most thought the responsibility lay elsewhere. The *only* person prepared to admit he had failed in any way was the secretary of defence, Allan Hawke, who offered his resignation when it became clear he should have pressed with the minister the issue of the misinterpreted photographs. None of them argued that their actions were political.

But perhaps there was too much passion, too great a desire to back up the story, and too little of the professional scepticism that is required. There are enough advocates in politics; public servants need to ask for the hard evidence. Outside Defence they did not treat the initial claim with any scepticism at all, even though it was based only on a train of phone calls. We need that balance and scepticism.

The *Public Service Act* 1999, passed by the Howard government, requires public servants to provide "frank, honest, comprehensive, accurate and timely advice". Accurate? Timely? It was not accurate, although for ministers the initial advice was certainly timely. But the correction was all too slow. As the chair of the select committee noted: "everyone builds an edifice of proof that the first accusation did not have to meet but the retraction does." Then the evidence has to prove that something did not happen. Every eyewitness account could be discounted because it did not prove that an incident did not occur out of sight. The requirements of the *Public Service Act* must surely cover the need for the facts to be accurate and, if they are not, for the story to be corrected clearly and unequivocally. Public servants must properly work within government policy. But within those limits they have a professional responsibility to ensure that processes work well, that advice is given and received, and that the facts are true. Timely and accurate? The correction was neither.

Ministerial Staff: At least in a constitutional sense, ministerial staff are out of control. They are beyond the supervision of parliament, and there are too many for them to be regarded as an extension of the ministers. The evidence suggests that they ring officers throughout the departments and demand answers—sometimes politely, sometimes peremptorily. They may or may not pass on all they know. Logically, they cannot tell everything; no minister or prime minister can absorb the information gained by an extensive staff. So they pick and choose.

With a nudge and a wink, the ministers may make it clear what they do not want to know. Even without it, advisers will be aware of what they should not pass on and conscious of what political spin is required. If the information they collect from the bureaucracy can be packaged so that the ministers present favourable stories, so much the better. Here, the justifications for the lack of change in the advice, or for not bothering the minister, came in all forms: their information always had to be checked; it was tea room gossip; we were waiting for a final report; we weren't satisfied that it was comprehensive; there was no formal advice. Of course. As *Yes Minister* so cleverly illustrated, for those who do not want to hear no answers are adequate. There are always questions unanswered. (The ones that were not asked, Sir Humphrey would chortle).

But we simply do not know what the advisers passed on, although we can assume they would protect the minister and the prime minister. Two examples indicate this. Scrafton told the prime minister that the video was inconclusive but, the prime minister insists, he did not mention the doubts about the whole affair that he had heard a month before. Jordana knew that the sources for the ONA report were probably ministerial media announcements. Could the prime minister have possibly defended his government with such vigour if he had been told that the ONA report was based on his own statements? Surely not, but by suggesting it might have been based on Defence reports the ONA fax of the night before left just enough doubt for the prime minister to use the report as evidence before the Press Club. What did the advisers pass on? Nothing, perhaps, of the doubts they both knew about. Even though Scrafton and Jordana are public servants on secondment and not partisan advisers, they too will absorb the need to protect the minister and the prime minister.

If staffers are intermediaries who control access to the minister, and indeed to the media, their position is significant. They work closely with the ministers; they are the last voice in their ears; they sieve and control advice from senior officials. They are no longer bit players. We need to hold them accountable.

Ministers and prime ministers: Are ministers and the prime minister accountable? There is one clear theme that runs throughout this case, one constant refrain: "we acted on advice", "we did not change our view because no one told us", "we believed what we were told", "we have not been formally told that the incident did not happen". "If you do not believe the navy, there is no hope," one press questioner was told. The ministers rode on the back of their advisers and the reluctance of Defence to correct a lie.

There is nothing new in ministers prefacing every statement with the comment that they had been advised of this or that. It provides the alibi: if it was not true it is not my fault; my advisers should have got it right the first time. Blame the officials; they cannot respond.

But how long should that alibi be allowed to last? In this case, the defence minister and his office were told the photos were wrong and that there were doubts about the whole story. They claim they asked for clarifying advice which was never provided. But it was convenient not to press hard, not to raise the issue again, and not to ask hard questions: the convenience of deniability. The unseen video provided the cover until the last week when the fig leaf of the ONA report and the appeals to the integrity of the ministers became the last resort. "Why would we lie?" they asked. For we must believe they are all honourable men.

The ministers and the prime minister *were* told in writing that children had been thrown overboard. But as the supports for the story fell away, they must have realised how flimsy the remaining edifice was. By emphasising the need for the initial advice to be revoked only by *formal advic*e, they allowed rumour, passing asides, and phone calls to be discounted. But the reliance on formal advice became more shrill as it became the only story left. It was true, in the literal sense. It was increasingly less persuasive as a defence.

So what is "the formal advice" that ministers required? It is easier, on the basis of this case, to say what it is not. It is not a conversation between ministers. Reith suggested to Howard in the last week that there might be doubts, but that was not enough for the story to be corrected. It is not, it seems, an oral briefing. Houston told Reith, but the minister wanted to wait till Barrie had returned before he accepted it, even though Houston was acting chief of the defence force. It is not the use of formal channels. Defence liaison told his superiors in Prime Minister and Cabinet in what he described as a formal brief, but it was disregarded as tea room gossip. Moore-Wilton later noted that "there are no written records or recollections that have come to light within the Department of Prime Minister and Cabinet to substantiate Commander King's evidence to the Senate Select Committee that he sought to *formally* [emphasis in original] advise officers … that information given to the Government in regard to 'children overboard' photographs was incorrect". He could not "accept the proposition that concerns were brought officially to the attention of PM&C management".

The list of negatives goes on. "Formal advice" is not just a conversation, as Silverstone had with Reith in Darwin, because that could be rejected as just a passing comment. It is not a warning in a written brief requested by the taskforce and delivered by higher strategic command: that was sent to a junior officer in the prime minister's department, and was not accompanied by a phone call to warn of its significance. It is not a warning to an adviser or a message on voicemail. Indeed the only advice that was given the sobriquet of "formal" in this whole affair was the initial advice in the paper sent to ministers on 7 October that stated without caveat that children had been thrown overboard, and *that* was based on a series of phone calls. Oral briefings, written comments, warnings at meetings, conversations: none constitute formal briefing. Secretary of defence Hawke did instruct that a formal brief be sent to the minister, but it was not.

"Formal advice", or the lack of it, has become the ever-useful fiction. It seems that it almost requires an official to state in advance that the advice about to be presented is "formal", rather like pronouncements of papal infallibility. But that is obviously absurd in an environment where records are fewer and when speed is demanded.

This litany suggests a study in ambiguity. With a few exceptions, formal advice is advice that people want to hear. If it raises doubts, it is not formal. Formal advice may be sought in the expectation it will not come, because there are some questions for which people do not want an answer *yet*, and if it did come it could never satisfy the demands and would be sent back for correction.

But more than that, some information may not be obtained because, deliberately, no one asks for it. It takes some discipline not to ask obvious questions. All the supports for the story—the photographs, the crew's statements, the video, the ONA report—were shown not to provide corroborating evidence. From that moment the obvious questions were: "Well, is there any evidence to support the story? Did it happen in the first place?" Yet in the last week of the campaign these may well be the questions that were never asked because no one wanted to know the answer. Plausible deniability could be retained only so long as they were not asked and the ministers, particularly the prime minister, were not explicitly told.

Yet the "I was advised" defence is, at best, weak. Why? First, because ministers do not just act on advice; they are elected to decide. The minister and his staff had no problem imposing a rigid media blackout on Defence against the experience and advice of the department. It could instruct the navy to act as the bulwark against refugees, a role the navy accepted as legitimate (albeit barely and uncomfortably). Indeed the history of the last decades is the story of the greater dominance of ministers over the detail of policy making and the increasing responsiveness of public servants (too much so, some critics believe) to ministerial command.

So for ministers then to hide behind the routine that "I was advised" is less than credible. As the questions flowed they could have demanded more detail. Reith might well say in February, from the security of retirement: "I think now, looking back on the whole situation, it would have been much better if we had a clear statement of what happened in writing before anyone had said anything." He is right. But he could also have asked for that statement as soon as doubts emerged, and demanded a same-day response. That would have killed the story stone dead. He preferred not to. The impression that emerges is one where the maintenance of fuzziness and doubt, the contested interpretations and the misunderstandings, suited the players. Nothing in writing, please. The rules are clear.

Second, the "I am advised" routine undercuts the core of accountability. Advisers are responsible to ministers. But here ministers say they are in the hands of officials. Neither takes responsibility, and a vacuum develops. Ministers took actions because advisers told them that was what was correct; advisers tell ministers and leave them to correct the record. And the public is misled, which can be useful during election time when ambiguity is needed and when the mirage can be retained just long enough to get to the polls. But it is a strategy that has strict time limits at other times in the political cycle. How often, on other occasions, do we hear ministers saying for weeks that "this is what I have been advised". Very seldom. Ministers are usually obliged to demand that facts be checked. Caretaker conventions did not preclude requests for these facts to be checked out. The tactic was suitable for the time and the circumstances. It may never have been spelt out; it was almost certainly not coordinated. But the players knew the game.

Does this mean that the system has failed us? At one level there is an uneasy feeling that all the actors were doing what they believed they should: assisting the government. Public servants provide information, going perhaps to the edge of the partisan divide but not (or not often) beyond it. The policy was in place; all they did was provide information and implement that policy, with the mindset that they must still support the government. Too little scepticism and distance at that time, perhaps, but within the rules and imbued with the caution created by the knowledge these will still be their political masters after the election is over. Why risk a career by being too forward in pushing unwelcome news?

Ministerial staff are often partisan, tough, impatient, and biased, sometimes arrogant, and they play to win. Their standing orders: confusion to the enemy (or the media); use officials; support the ministers. There have always been enough of them who fit this caricature to make the account in this case unsurprising. Ministers, meanwhile, are precise in their use of language, skilful in their operation of the systems; they know when to use alibis, cut outs, and the perennial "I am advised ..."

In other words, it's business as usual. Indeed, no one has been blamed for these incidents, and several actors have been promoted. It is true that some reputations among peers may be damaged as the more dramatic somersaults and barrages of forgetfulness are greeted with derision. But in general we can only assume that many of those in government cannot see what the fuss is about. It was just executive prerogative and party politics at work.

The prime minister tells us that he did not know that the story was untrue. But he was surrounded by those who knew, or should have known, that there were doubts. He talked to the defence minister who had been told a month before of the ambiguities, and explicitly by Houston of the doubts about the event itself. He talked to Scrafton about the video, but Scrafton had known for a month that Defence had doubts and did not tell him about them. Jordana knew that the ONA report was not really evidence, and knew of the doubts expressed and the tea room gossip. Officers in his department had been told a month before that there was no documentary evidence, that the photos were misrepresented, and that there were no women in the water on 7 October even though the photos showed women. They had been sent briefs that never mentioned the event. If the department did not *formally* know, it should have. All these people knew or should have known. Just about everyone in Defence knew except the chief of the defence force, who was aware of doubts but did not change his advice.

The prime minister has the largest office in history, and it is dedicated to providing him with information. In his initial comment to the media, he used the caveat: "If these reports are true." He later said he would ask for checks to be made. If they were, he insists he was never told the outcome. The advisers never told him and he never pressed them. In the last week of the campaign his defence on ABC-TV's *Lateline* was, in effect, "this is what we were advised;, I have been told nothing else; I believe the navy and we are all honourable men".

How do we read this situation? A canny controlling prime minister not told about a story that covered the front pages? It could be Murphy's law—that is, a stuff-up. But we might then expect someone to be held accountable for the mess; no one has been.

Or it could be a machine working at its best, a machine designed to protect and promote the government. Serving the government is what the public service does. No one wants the prime minister to have to correct himself during an election campaign, particularly on so central an issue. So the prime minister is protected by his ministers, his office, and his department. Pleading a lack of clear advice, emphasising the uncertainty, they pass on nothing. "Don't tell the prime minister" must be the prevailing rule. Howard said in February that if he had "received contrary advice, I would have made that contrary advice public". His staff knew better than to face him with that alternative.

But there is still the concern that for a month the Australian people were not told they had been misled. That should concern us all. There are many excuses but few reasons. We need an acceptance of accountability somewhere in the system, an appreciation that such a situation is not desirable. We have been given it almost nowhere. We should reasonably expect that senior officials will ensure that ministers are not misled or, if they are, that the correct facts will be given as a matter of urgency. We should expect that, after the first cautious statement, ministers will know what is true because they demanded the facts were checked, again as a matter of urgency. If the system failed, we need someone who takes responsibility. If this is a system that was working as participants believed it should, the rest of us should be worried.

Perhaps we need a change of attitude, one closer to that of

the man from whom Howard got his middle name: Winston Churchill. Certainly he was always partisan, blithely opportunistic, and often cynical. But he was prepared to take responsibility. When told of the loss of Singapore and the weakness of its defences, he is said to have commented: "I did not know, I was not told, I should have asked."

That's accountability. It accepts that public servants should check and tell. It accepts that ministers should ask. I'd like to see that.

Sources

This book is based mainly on evidence provided to two Senate committees. The Senate Estimates Committee held hearings in February 2002. The Senate Select Committee on a Certain Maritime Incident held a series of hearings from March to June.

Two internal reports were written on the incident. The routine inquiry conducted by Major General Roger Powell reported to the chief of defence force. The *Investigation into Advice Provided to Ministers on SIEV 4* was commissioned by the secretary of the Department of the Prime Minister and Cabinet at the request of the prime minister. It was undertaken by Jennifer Bryant, assistant secretary of education and immigration branch of the social policy division. Both reports were tabled in parliament by the prime minister; both were based a number of witness statements and supporting documents, all of which were given to the select committee and released to the public. Transcripts of hearings, witness statements, and supporting documentation run to hundreds of pages. All quotations in the book are drawn from these sources unless otherwise stated.

In addition I have drawn on material from earlier studies I have undertaken. They include: *Politics and Policy in Australia* (with Geoffrey Hawker and R.F.I. Smith), 1979; *Can Ministers Cope?* (with Michelle Grattan), 1981; *Malcolm Fraser, Prime Minister*, 1989); and *Australia's Mandarins*, 2001.

The study on caretaker conventions was "Rethinking Caretaker Conventions for Australian Governments", by G. Davis, A. Ling, B. Scales, and R. Wilkins, *Australian Journal of Public Administration*, 60(3), pages 11–26.

Acknowledgements

I want to thank Anne Tiernan for assisting in the collection of the data for this study, for mastering the intricacies of the internet in a way I could never learn, and for reading the manuscript. Rod Rhodes, Philip Selth, Bron Stevens, and John Uhr also read the text and provided constructive suggestions. Olwen Schubert designed the diagram.

Geoff Pryor was wonderfully generous in allowing us to reproduce his cartoons from the *Canberra Times*. He also gave us one original cartoon, reproduced here on page 44.

Peter Browne was a meticulous editor and constant encouragement. The book was his idea, but he can't be blamed for the result.

Finally, and as ever, I want to thank all those public servants, past and present, who have spent time over the years talking about their roles and responsibilities. If there are insights of value in the essay they are due to you, even if, of course, you may not recognise them.